The Business Fitness Revolution

by Brad Tornberg

Dedicated to my children Rachel, Erica and Haley Tornberg and my grandchild Cole Siracuse.

ISBN-13: 978-1500953997
ISBN-10: 1500953997

Introduction

I wrote this book because as a technology and marketing consultant, I fix problems for a living. Most of my clients consider me a troubleshooter who gets to the root cause of their issues. And that's exactly how I want you to view this book—as a way to diagnose and fix your currently unhealthy business. Notice I said "unhealthy" instead of "struggling," "failing," or even "poorly performing." That's because my book promotes the idea that healthy businesses are run by healthy business owners and CEOs. Sounds too simple, doesn't it? But it's true; your business's health is a reflection of your human body's health.

A long time ago, I transitioned from being employed by a kaleidoscope of businesses (small and large, and mostly technology-related) to running my own business. The Business Fitness Revolution is the summation of 30 years' worth of working with clients and observing how they do what they do. I've seen it all: I've worked with small businesses, family businesses, and growing businesses going through cultural changes as the result of a merger or acquisition.

To me, this book is a printed legacy I'm passing on to both current and future entrepreneurs so they can learn from my business mistakes (and companion solutions). I know I can help you either avoid unhealthy business habits or treat and heal them if you've already ignored all the warning signs. All the processes in place that allow your business to function are equal to all the systems in your body that keep you alive and well. So let's talk more about your health and how it relates to business fitness.

As a business owner, principal or CEO, it's time you stop frantically scurrying to douse fires and take a hard look at yourself. Do this in front of a mirror if you want to be brutally honest about it. You need to realize you may not be in the best physical health and that your personal health has a cascading effect on your company. If you're not in good shape, how can you lead, and how can you expect your people to happily follow your leadership? This question has a painfully simple answer: Your current expectations are completely misguided. Don't look for any apologies from me regarding this statement. You'll just have to keep reading!

Because YOU have health issues, your problems drip down from the top and seep throughout your entire organization. When unhealthy business habits spread to the lowest employee on your totem pole, efficiency stops, and things don't get fixed. Later in this book, I'll explain in detail my People-Process-Technology triangle (PPT) of business fitness health. As your company's leader, when you change one angle of the PPT triangle, you also need to adjust the other two angles to maintain a healthy equilibrium. For now, all you need to know is that you are the starting point to your company's better health. Even more important, you have to be willing to admit you have a problem, and you have to want to heal yourself first. Your health may be an indicator of larger issues festering within your business. It's just like going to the doctor because you don't feel well; you think it's one thing, but it turns out to be another issue.

The trickle-down effect of your not-so-glowing health reveals itself as unfortunate symptoms exhibited by your employees: malaise and lethargy on the job, bad attitudes, bad customer service, a high turnover rate, and slow business or project transaction time. When I talk about health, I'm not just referring to elements of physical fitness (strength training, cardio workouts, yoga and Pilates, etc.). I'm also including mental fitness (meditation, rest and relaxation, technology breaks, etc.), nutrition, and lifestyle balance in my equation of overall health. If you're not in good physical and mental shape, I guarantee you're not agile enough to handle the stress of running a business. You need to convert yourself and your dysfunctional organization into an efficient, healthy organism.

Have you turned into what I refer to as a "popcorn leader?" This is a business owner or CEO who constantly delegates important tasks to someone else, pops into someone's office for a few minutes to stir things up, and then leaves without offering any clear plan or action steps. Popcorn leaders keep popping away, but they don't give their people the time they deserve, and they don't resolve the internal chaos they themselves ignite. This style of leadership indicates less than optimal business fitness; you do not want to be this person. It's time to step away from the C-level salt shaker (and artificial butter flavoring) and end this dysfunctional behavior.

When a new client hires me as their technology and marketing consultant, I always meet first with the company's top leader. I do so because usually, that's where change needs to start before the company's employees are even willing to accept and adapt to change. It is no joke that when I first collaborate with a business's CEO or owner, I'll strongly counsel starting an exercise/training program if they're not at optimal health. Why? Because owners are a reflection of their business, and without good health, neither can perform at full throttle. If you want the agility and endurance necessary for long-term success, then business fitness is the only viable path to follow.

I'm not saying this is easy—my business fitness regimen is both evolutionary and revolutionary. That's why I gave my book the title you see on the cover. Once you've read the entire book, perhaps you'll start thinking like a reformed smoker who first struggled to quit, but then tired of the inconvenience of it all and the peer pressure. Like the ex-smoker, you'll realize the change needed (to heal your business) must start with you, or it will never happen. Once I have your buy-in and you take control of your own health, you'll begin to notice that most of the people in your company admire your willingness to change, so they will change too. This is the power of momentum by the masses—it can permanently alter your business's culture and performance for the better. While most employees will adapt to the new, positive energy lifting your business to greater success, there will be some who refuse to change. This passive resistance can sabotage your company's improving health. Don't worry about these straggling outliers—they will either adapt or leave. Everyone who remains an employee with your company will benefit.

If you are thriving, your business will also thrive. Because your business's symptoms may not indicate the actual "illness," I look to you first as the actual "thermometer" of your company. Once you concede your health and that of your business are codependent, each chapter in this book will ring true for you. At the risk of using too vivid a metaphor, when a fish's head is cut off, the body thrashes around for a few floundering seconds; you know what happens next. This book will help prevent you and your business from becoming decapitated fish heads...

The Business Fitness Revolution is designed to be an actionable tool for improving your business's health. But the book is just one part of an overall strategy nudging you toward your healthier lifestyle and leadership style. Other resources soon to be available as you pursue optimal business health include: the Business Fitness Workout (yes, I do mean physical exercise), self-assessment quizzes, and Business Fitness workbooks for monitoring your progress. I will also offer personal mentoring groups for those of you who desire a total-fitness lifestyle and want to have some fun while you're healing your business.

Here's a preview of the chapters awaiting your curiosity and reading attention:
Chapter One: The Brain and Central Nervous System
Chapter Two: The Stomach and Digestive System
Chapter Three: The Optical (Eyes) System
Chapter Four: The Auditory System (Ears)
Chapter Five: The Vocal Cords/Resonator System (Voice)
Chapter Six: The Cardiovascular System
Chapter Seven: The Circulatory System
Chapter Eight: The Muscular System
Chapter Nine: The Skeletal System
Chapter Ten: The Respiratory System
Chapter Eleven: Business Nutrition and the Immune System
Chapter Twelve: The Total Business Body

Don't say you haven't been warned that the business fitness revolution is coming. This will be a new way of assessing and addressing your business woes, that's for sure. You'll soon learn how to listen to your business body and train your senses regarding when it feels pain and when it feels well.

Remember, your personal health comes first. Without you, there is no business. Maybe I am overdramatizing a bit; it's possible your business could continue to survive its current rundown state. But without optimal health, you won't be around to enjoy your business's startling changeover and success. If you already maintain a lifestyle full of physical and mental wellness, consider this book a road map for converting your employees to better health and a happier work life. Either way, I invite you to join my revolution and not get left behind.

Chapter One: The Business Brain and Central Nervous System

Let's start with your brain and Central Nervous System, since these are where your business messages originate and get disseminated to the rest of your business's body. Just like some unfortunate soul who's been in an accident and now has limited brain capacity, your business brain may be struggling to send out the proper messages that can guide your business to optimal health. Think about how powerful your brain truly is—it's the keeper of your emotions, your personal philosophy, your business ideologies and how you go to market with your products/services, and so on.

If your business has a brain, then you, as the leader, are the brain stem. Just like the brain stem connects the rest of your brain to its spinal cord, you connect your employees to your company: how they should act, how things get done, etc. The brain stem controls all the automatic functions that keep a body alive (breathing, digestion of food, blood circulation). You're also responsible for sorting through the massive amount of messages sent back and forth between the brain and the rest of your body. No wonder being a CEO or business owner is so demanding—you have to process endless stimuli.

So your brain comes up with surefire ways to improve operational processes, but how does your message get sent to the furthest reaches of your business? Think of your Central Nervous System (CNS—no, not Crosby, Nash and Stills!) as your business's internal version of that childhood favorite, the telephone game (aka "Whisper Down the Lane"). The CNS does much heavy lifting to create the culture of how your company works.

There are many ways to spread a message these days (e-mail, phone, text messages, etc.), but how effective is your CNS? When Uma Thurman's character in the movie *Kill Bill (Vol. 1)* woke up from her coma, her body wasn't functioning too well. Through sheer will (and Quentin Tarantino's direction), her brain convinced her CNS to "wiggle your big toe." If your message delivery system is short-circuited in any way, then your business body isn't functioning at 100%.

Together, your brain and CNS are the keys to your company's mental health. A damaged business brain/CNS partnership indicates an idea not getting properly dispersed companywide. Need to be convinced of this? I can't offer you any better proof than one of the most profound lines from a famous Pink Floyd song, "Brain Damage": "And if the band you're in starts playing different tunes, I'll see you on the dark side of the moon." The different tunes are your company's mixed-up messages. I don't think the "dark side of the moon" reference needs any explanation from a business perspective…

In my honest opinion, we've all gotten away from effective verbal communication by drifting toward a bad business habit: instant gratification. I'm the first to admit I can't imagine living without my 21st century e-mail, texting, and social media posting options. But according to Marshall McLuhan way back in the 1960s, "the medium is the message." It's great to communicate quickly with rapid-fire ease, but is the message you send the same one received? A healthy CNS relates well to the Japanese belief in "kaizen," or continuous improvement. How you collect and distribute information within your company is vital to successful communication. You could learn a lot about continuous improvement from The Walt Disney Company, a prime example of a business with a strong, adaptable CNS.

A lot of the frustration regarding your internal communication stems from your employees feeling either less than equal to you or left out from the decision-making process. When these short-circuited communication issues finally reach you, perhaps you'll admit (to your people, to yourself) that you had no idea your employees felt this way. This is a sure sign of a malfunctioning CNS. Another signal of CNS trouble is the bad assumption that everyone in your company feels the same level of dedication and love as you do for your "business child."

If you follow my business brain theory, you'll instinctively understand that different parts of your brain are better suited for accomplishing different tasks. For example, you might be good at geography and be able to rattle off the capitals of all the Baltic nations. But then I'll throw a simple math equation at you ($55 + 44 = ?$), and perhaps you freeze. Same brain, same CNS, so what's the problem? By developing different ways of communicating with your employees, depending on your end goal, you'll find yourself either consolidating or expanding your messages. Once you figure out optimal ways of sharing important information with your people internally, your business brain and CNS will run at 100%. Of course, your reaction time and agility also impact this part of your business body's functionality...

When I mention your brain's reaction time, I'm talking about how quickly you respond to the events and situations that happen all around you. These occurrences can be positive (a new product taking off like a fireworks finale) or negative (a public relations fiasco you never saw coming). Think about how you would react to being in a car accident. Do you become the deer paralyzed by the oncoming headlights of the other vehicle, or do you (if able) call the police, look for any witnesses at the scene, and check on the other people involved?

Comparable business scenarios requiring your best reaction time include: changing your business's direction, expanding your business, buying a business, or deciding to allow your business to be acquired. This may sound harsh, but companies fail and go out of business because they don't react well to change of any kind (financial, technological, etc.). As a function of your business brain, reaction time is critical to fending off your competitors' efforts to win and your survival.

While reaction time equates to speed, agility equates to how effectively you turn once you spot something that can't be ignored. It's great to have a reaction time that demonstrates bold decisiveness. But if you make the wrong decision, leading to costly or irreversible damage to your company, your agility is lacking, which can be fatal. Both proper reaction time and agility affect your business brain's success. Never disregard them, unless you run your company by the Clint Eastwood/Dirty Harry philosophy of random probability: "You've got to ask yourself one question: 'Do I feel lucky?' Well do you, punk?" Now that I've introduced a .44 Magnum handgun into the discussion, let's move on to your business smarts, why projects fail, and acceptance/usage of technology within your company...

Any internal project starts at the top with your executive brain. Any project's success relies upon your support, your being behind it. The CEO is the foundation and source of all key buy-in within a company, so your business brain needs to be tuned in and turned ON! In all the years I've been a business consultant, I've observed too many times the number one reason why projects fail. Are you ready for this unbelievable bombshell? Your company's projects fail when you and your people aren't communicating. The corollary is that projects fail when management changes direction, but neglects to communicate it well (or at all) to the people directly responsible for the necessary grunt work.

This bad communication leads to mixed messages and confusion. Once your business gets trapped in a communicative death spiral, your employees get paranoid, productivity and creativity slide, and your business heart and stomach are in need of some serious triage. Bad communication doesn't just imperil project success—it also undermines your business's optimal health. Your business brain must move forward and follow through on the many messages it processes. Without action, you miss out on successful decision-making and important opportunities. Is it possible your business brain underestimated the manpower or effort needed for a particular project?

I think of this as that scene in an action film when the hero needs to escape some "badass" chasing him with a gun. You know—he's on an urban rooftop, comes to a ledge, and he eyeballs the space between the ledge and that of the next building's rooftop. His adrenaline pumping, he thinks he can make it. (And then, look at that, he does!) But running your business isn't like filming a movie scene. When you need to jump between two buildings to move a project forward, do you listen to your brain, or do you let the rest of your business body take over and decide for you?

Your brain should sense that your body is about to make a big mistake and pull you back. What I mean is this: You should change direction, rest a bit, and then correct the situation with proper action. Don't jump! Just like your "eyes can be bigger than your stomach," your business body can be bigger than your project, so the brain must intercede and prevent catastrophe.

Your attitude regarding the importance of managing the project well also matters to its success or failure. When it comes to project management, do you want a graduate-level brain in charge, or are you leaving your company's most important client/account in the hands of a fourth-grade-level brain? This is not the time to follow directions for a model-building kit and then find you have a few screws and odd pieces left over afterward. Your fully functioning brain should realize that proper project management inevitably involves computers and technology to make your business body smarter and more efficient.

A key take-home for your business brain is that technology needs to be viewed and used as a tool, not as a task. If you use technology properly, you should get smarter, and it should help remove emotions and gut instinct from your business decisions. Technology is a means to becoming agile and proactive, rather than reactive. Your proactive brain uses technology as a tool to plan. But your reactive brain gets trapped by technology-related tasks. It's as if you're participating in a mental Chinese fire drill at a stoplight, but you panic. Your brain must decide whether technology is your friend or your foe!

Healthy companies (and their brains) always find ways to introduce technology at all levels within the organization. You need to find out which hardware/software training methods work best for your people. Whether it's an offsite company class, online tutorials, self-training in the privacy of an office or one-on-one hand holding, technology should be promoted as an effective tool, not a feared task. Of course, some companies wield technology as a way to weed out their weakest users. Let's take a closer look at how technology functions in an unhealthy business.

Without fail, my clients running less-than-healthy businesses have an IT department (or an IT person) making employees' lives miserable by operating as a gatekeeping fiefdom. The IT director or manager becomes the data "border patrol" within the company. Once data checks in, it's not so easy for your employees to check it out. Yes, you should be visualizing the infamous Black Flag Roach Motel™ right now. Not a comforting metaphor to associate with your beloved company, is it?

Here's something so important to believe that I want you to memorize it: Your IT department should serve one client – your business. If someone submits a work order or request to your IT department but it takes weeks or months for the issue to be resolved, IT will get a bad reputation within your company. Your CIO will be feared, the pain of not being able to fulfill everyday business needs will be real, and oh yes, that pain will spread like a stomach virus at an elementary school. Don't let this happen…

Here's another truism I want you to accept: Healthy businesses embrace technology and understand that it's an investment, not an expense. If you do nothing but emit trickle-down messages of "Let's process more data with less (or obsolete) technology" to your IT staff and employees, you're setting up the entire enterprise for failure. Don't be that thought(less) leader! If you haven't sent any employees to a technical training class within the past three years, something is wrong with your business brain. By investing in your employees' technological knowledge and continuing education, you ensure this aspect of business agility.

And while we're discussing technology, I'll go ahead and broach the hot topic of social media usage by your employees. Healthy companies empower their people to use LinkedIn, Facebook, Twitter, YouTube, Pinterest, and other platforms in a good way without compromising or imposing on anyone's personal life. It's really quite simple. If social media is a part of your business body, you need to develop straightforward policies and procedures that everyone can understand and implement the first time these rules are shared.

I'll push this a little further. Face your social media fears and cure them, don't put your employees on lockdown. This will just cause them to grumble about their lack of freedom. Also, you'll be setting them up for failure because they can't fully function (and compete!) on behalf of YOUR company. By embracing social media, you provide your people another way to listen to both customers and competitors. Take a little bite right now – if you've never set up any Google Alerts regarding your products, services, or competition, go to http://www.google.com/alerts and create some based on your industry keywords. If you don't yet have a Google account, get going and create one today.

Also, are you paying attention to social media's ever-evolving adoption curve? In 2010, consumers began their ascent by shopping online and engaging in online communities. Now in 2013, most corporate leaders no longer view social media as a gimmick. They've stopped frightening themselves with the false assumption that their employees use social media to shop 24/7 and watch pornography! Instead, businesses are rolling these online platforms into their marketing mix. According to John Jantsch of Duct Tape Marketing, the traditional sales funnel has been permanently altered by social media. Instead of cold calling (and forcing your prospects to jump through qualifying hoops), your selling success now relies upon the people in your online/offline communities who know, like, and trust you.

By 2025, I believe those companies with viable online models will finally unlock the secrets of digital monetization and generate a percentage of their business through social media and blogging. Let's be honest—both e-mail marketing and social media are now integrated aspects of your business's health. If you're not optimizing your employees' use of social media platforms, I can guarantee your competitors are doing so and will jump ahead of you. Embrace social media now, listen well, and engage sincerely in a timely manner. [Please note: Certain industries, like the financial services sector, aren't a great fit with social media usage, due to compliance and regulatory restrictions.]

Many of my clients own family-run companies. So, I've earned the right to talk about this type of business owner's brain, which can be quite dysfunctional. The family business brain is always more intense and carries more psychological weight. That's because it's emotionally attached to people such as a spouse, a son/daughter, or other assorted relatives. Thus, certain family-run business employees are a part of the inner circle. They never feel like they're on the outside looking in, their noses pressed up against the front window.

One noticeably different characteristic of this business type is the family members' internal perspective. If you own a family business, you know what I'm talking about. Even though family members may tear each other up verbally, they can still talk and work together the next day as if nothing happened. This craziness (or *mishegoss*, as my Jewish clients call it) that seems normal to you when you're yelling at your kid or sibling for doing something without your permission seems bizarre to nonfamily employees. These "outsiders" begin to wonder if you'll treat them in the same way on a regular basis. Not a good vibe to spread (unintentionally) throughout your long-term livelihood...

Another personal observation regarding family-run businesses is that when the entrepreneurial spirit skips a generation, trouble lies ahead. The not-particularly-interested heir apparent (who is slated to take over the business) breeds resentment among all your nonfamily employees. There's also a lot of sales staff turnover, especially when the family business owner doesn't have any clear structure in place. Then there's what I call the "shield of invincibility." This is the (not completely misguided) perception that family members working for the business won't be fired because a feeling of entitlement buffers them from this common fear.

Almost all of the family businesses I work with "get broken" because of the owner. When the business has enough layers to it, this lessens the pain, but the owner's dysfunctional brain still manages to muck it up for both family and non-family employees. Just like someone you know with an addiction (to alcohol, to gambling, to hoarding), the family business owner needs to admit there's a problem before any healing can begin.

When I work with a family business, my most important role tends to be that of impartial referee. If anything I've described here sounds like your family business, it's time to take that honest look in the mirror. Ask your "outside" employees to put together their internal "we hate when this happens" list. Don't be so stubborn about seeking third-party help to remediate your misfiring brain and CNS. The quickest way to get your family enterprise healthy is to admit your problem, take on a real, tangible business structure, and then prepare to adapt to the coming changes. If you, as Mama or Papa Smurf, make ALL the critical decisions for your business, you are the bottleneck clogging your company's pipes. Once you begin trusting nonfamily staff to also share in the decision-making process, your company will start "living" a healthier life.

Some final advice about family businesses: Don't treat your cash flow as if it's your own personal piggy bank. Once your nonfamily employees catch on that you and your loved ones get more than your fair share of vacations, new cars and other shiny things, animosity will grow like mold after a basement's flooding. Avoid this temptation if you can. Purposefully create a path to financial success for those employees showing up five days a week who aren't family members. Enough said...

I promised you in my Introduction I would elaborate on my People-Process-Technology triangle (PPT). This seems the right place to do it. Any dysfunctional part of your business's body requiring an adjustment or fix falls into at least one of these three categories (People, Process, or Technology).

The People component of my triangle is a common, self-inflicted business problem. Either (some of) your people aren't capable of doing the job they were hired to do, or they're capable, but drowning in their project volume. In other words, it's the wrong manpower versus not enough manpower. Not having the right employees in place means you're allowing The Peter Principle to populate your business with a bunch of nice people who aren't qualified to hold their jobs, yet they continue to climb up through your organization. If this isn't a sure sign of an unhealthy business, I don't know what is.

The Process component is simply how things get done (or don't get done) within your company. Processes are the rules, the policies and procedures, the corporate decisions clearly communicated to your people so they don't have to waste valuable work time figuring out how you expect them to function successfully each day. Similar to the manpower issue, an unhealthy business either has the wrong processes in place or not enough of them (i.e., process gaps). Once I start working with a new client, I'll know within a few weeks whether or not process gaps exist just by observing repetitive inefficiencies each time I'm on-site.

I already delved into the triangle's Technology component a bit earlier in this chapter. It comes down to this: Is technology properly used and supported within your business, or is it adding time and frustration to your employees' work lives? Is technology a dreaded task within your organization, or is it an understood and well-used tool? Software is flexible and can be programmed to innovate and create, but it's fallible, so you need to know where your technology gaps are and modify them on a regular basis.

By viewing your business through my People-Process-Technology prism, you will realize your internal problems are multidimensional. Even if you clearly identify a serious People problem, this one aspect of the PPT triangle is interrelated with your Process and Technology issues. It's never just a one-dimensional challenge—when you change one angle in the triangle, you must assess and adjust the other two angles to maintain equilibrium. Your business brain is unhealthy when you're focused on only one variable of the triangle, rather than all three components. For those of you wondering what fills in the PPT triangle: it's money, of course (i.e., your profits)!

Have you ever heard of "ceteris paribus?" It's a Latin phrase that translates into English as something you have heard before: "all other things being equal." But in the business world, there's no such thing as everything else remaining constant. You know as a business owner your path to success always changes and moves. Your company is an expensive version of three-dimensional chess. And when it's healthy, your people can move up and down, sideways and diagonally, just as if they're riding in Willy Wonka's glass elevator.

A corollary to my PPT triangle is what I call the Project Management triangle. Whether large or small, complicated or simple, your company is driven to success or failure by its projects. The angles of the Project Management triangle are: Time/Due Date, Money (invested into the project), and People/Manpower. Again, when you change one angle in this triangle, you must adjust the other angles, or your project management process will never achieve optimal health. It's all about cause and effect, just like finding out what happens when you ingest some medication to rid your body of an undesired illness. Choose your business medicine wisely!

Chapter One Story:

Once upon a time, I was hired by a family business owned by two brothers to handle their technology issues. But their real stumbling point turned out to be a serious people problem. These two brothers never spoke to each other! Additionally, I quickly discovered that both gentlemen had vastly different agendas regarding their business. Stunned by the seriousness of this dysfunctional relationship, I drew up and submitted a letter of engagement to my new client. The letter stated that for the next two weeks, I would interview each brother separately. I decided to function as a "corporate psychologist" so I could get to the root cause of their unhealthy (and separated-at-birth) business brain.

What I uncovered was a real shocker. The reason for this long-term rift between two adult brothers stemmed from a childhood incident involving money. The long-ago disagreement created such resentment between them that it was crippling their here-and-now business! While I was relieved to find out none of the company's employees knew about this situation, I realized I needed to heal the brothers' trust issues before I could tackle their internal technology challenges. So, I had the one brother pay back his childhood debt to the other brother.

The initial solution required some basic communication (long overdue, I'd say) to purge two business co-owners' dysfunctional brains. Once we got past the interpersonal roadblock, I helped this company double its revenue over the next three years. Sometimes it's a small thing festering over time that can derail any business's brain, family owned or not.

Chapter Two: The Stomach and Digestive System

In this chapter we'll assess how well you digest all the information entering your organization and how effectively you eliminate the waste by-products. Without getting ourselves into a repulsive discussion, let's have an honest conversation about your business stomach and digestive system (aka your business colon).

There's no escaping your physical stomach and colon—the phrase "you are what you eat" tends to be a revealing (and true) statement. But your business "gut" relies on a combination of hard facts and intuition for propelling you toward good decision-making. Similar to the way your stomach churns up whatever you decide to put into your body for nutrition, your business stomach breaks down a ton of information for your business gut to digest and process. Processed information should lead to decisions being made on a daily basis, but how does the information get dispersed throughout your company? Once the information is consumed (I sure hope it was tasty going down your esophagus), what do you do with it? How do you move it forward or in different directions where it's needed most? Two simple words: digestive enzymes.

All the information that flows into your employees' desktop or laptop (or tablet) computers via spreadsheets, CRM databases and the like is broken down into manageable pieces by a variety of digestive enzymes. Your physical stomach uses gastric enzymes such as pepsinogen (the main gastric enzyme), hydrochloric acid (strong stuff, this one) and mucin (protects the stomach's lining) to winnow out nutrients from that Chinese take-out meal you ate way too late last night. But the digestive enzymes sorting and processing all the data swallowed whole by your IT systems are your people.

Before you make any snap judgments regarding my comparison of complex proteins to your most valued talent, ride along with me for a paragraph or two. Each gastric acid in your stomach accomplishes something different before that gourmet meal you ate is sent to your digestive tract. So it makes sense that the many employee types and personalities working for you each add something different to your internal decision-making process. You don't want to rely on one digestive enzyme to understand and intuit the nuances of each important business decision. No, you need the proper mix of enzymes (your people) so that differing points of view are allowed to contribute to and strengthen each particular decision.

Here's what I know to be true: My clients tend to make bad decisions when the right person isn't asked to add his or her unique digestive enzyme into the mix. Just like Charlton Heston uttering his famous last line in the futuristic movie *Soylent Green* ("Soylent Green is people!"), I must passionately state that in the business body, digestive enzymes are people!

We've established that bringing as many different perspectives as possible into your decision process shields you from too myopic a point of view (namely, you). The other part of information processing and decision making involves your intuition. Your company's nutritional needs equate to your getting better over time at disseminating the right information to the right people. Efficient processing of your daily nutritional intake leads to quicker, better decisions and answers. As a result of all this digestive activity, you can take action before your competitors. But you should also put corrective measures into place to turnaround bad decisions when some rogue "junk food" sneaks into your business stomach. And don't tell me this would never happen at your company, because it already has (and you know it).

Nowadays, the IT world is all aflutter regarding the buzz phrase "Big Data." According to a March 2013 *New York Times* article, "Today, many experts predict that the next wave will be driven by technologies that fly under the banner of Big Data – data including Web pages, browsing habits, sensor signals, smartphone location trails and genomic information, combined with clever software to make sense of it all." A healthy business stomach is always ready to process these varying streams of real-time and descriptive data (so the business brain can know everything it needs to about its competition). If you've got the right balance of digestive enzymes working for you, your stomach can break down and process large quantities of information without getting indigestion (or propelling you to reach for a bottle of something pink or in tablet form). Once you've properly digested a competitive meal or two, consider using the SWOT analysis method (Strengths, Weaknesses, Opportunities, Threats) to the assess information before making decisions.

I realize I mentioned junk food without giving you a stern lecture, so we should briefly discuss your informational snacking habits. You've probably read or heard that the ideal food plan is to eat five or six small meals throughout your 12-to-16-hour meal cycle. Some nutritionists and dieticians refer to this method as "grazing." Perhaps this is good advice if each mini-meal contains nothing but highly nutritional foods like vegetables, fruits, lean protein, and barely-processed grains. However, you should beware overloading your people with too many e-mails, too many meetings, and too many memos or reports in between their efforts to process the information that adds value to your business.

In the physical world, snacking in between those healthy meals will slow down your metabolism and lead to weight gain; why would you want to inflict such punishment on your employees every day? The answer to my rhetorical question: You wouldn't want to do this! Allow your metaphorical digestive enzymes to do what you hired them to do (be successful so your business thrives and grows). Let them focus on breaking down the information given to them quickly and effectively. So lay off the snacks (both the informational and the bagged or boxed ones)...

Information is the nutrition processed by your business stomach, but how can you as a healthy business owner anticipate which pieces and bits of data are most important to good decision making? How best to proactively assess your internal issues before decisions go badly for you? Well, it's vital to have your systems in place—I'm referring back to my People-Process-Technology triangle from Chapter One. You need to know who is responsible for what information stream and why your people are collecting the information flowing into your data systems. Having healthy systems and efficient processes in place requires cleaning out your overstuffed "closets" every couple of months. You need to decide what stays and what goes.

My basic model for healthy consumption of information goes like this: intake it, process and analyze it, disseminate and utilize the good/necessary data, and eliminate the bad/unnecessary data. But don't bag up the unnecessary data and donate it to Goodwill or the Salvation Army—scour it out of existence. This is a simple enough plan, right? Remember though, there's the People angle of my PPT triangle. You need good, competent people in place to handle your systems and information. If the right people aren't on the job, replace them with people who fit into place like missing pieces of a jigsaw puzzle.

Here's some advice I want you to memorize: be lean. I'll say it again – BE LEAN! Information should get sent to the right people who can do something useful or proactive with it. Meetings are for making decisions quickly, not for sermonizing or wasting valuable thinking and doing time. Too many meetings aren't good for your people's processing capabilities—they just slow down your company's overall metabolism. Put your company on a lean meeting diet, starting today.

Think about this: If you don't eliminate waste quickly and properly (we'll get to that), it goes directly to your fat cells, which leads to weight gain. Do you want your company bloated by laziness and apathy, which ends up costing you more money, or do you want to own a healthy, lean business? You are what you eat, and so is your business. Do you remember those diet calendars from the 1970s featuring a gal named Bridget? She was so morbidly obese; I doubt she could move any faster than a three-toed sloth. Don't be the overweight person on a no-longer-funny novelty calendar—be lean.

Because your competitive landscape changes quarterly, it's also important to check your information frequency every few months. You must have good listening tools in place for an accurate look at your position in the marketplace. The value of good information is invaluable, especially feedback from your customers – both positive and negative. Don't keep eating "bad information" when your stomach is telling you it's not good for your company.

And it's not enough to distinguish between good and bad information – how quickly your employees process data also enhances the company's digestive health. You have many resources available to you for increasing information processing agility. Again, doing a SWOT analysis when you're stuck in a decision pothole will clarify all aspects of the issue and propel you to take action. A Customer Relationship Management (CRM) database is a comfortable resting place for basic customer data, but scaling up to use Anything Relationship Management (xRM) records is a more strategic approach that allows your people access to competitive information. You should be tracking your competitors' pricing strategies and how they execute marketing campaigns. Implementing secret shoppers is an innovative way to find out what your company is doing quite well or poorly if you're a retailer. Become your own toughest critic to better position your company in the marketplace.

By processing information well and being able to do it quickly enough, you'll find areas of opportunity (the "O" in your SWOT analysis) where you can leapfrog past your competition successfully. Put all those feedback surveys you ask customers to fill out to good use in a meaningful way. Don't be afraid to "open the kimono" to the rest of the world by admitting your mistakes and doing so quickly.

Again, the purpose of digesting your information properly and getting rid of what you don't need (including unnecessary people) is to keep your organization lean. No one wants to be told they're skinny when actually, they're overweight. Sometimes we need to face the truth so we can take care of things and fix what is making us unhealthy. Others' perceptions of your business are important. We all want to be slim and healthy, so retaining only the information that strengthens you is critical. As long as you're gaining muscle instead of fat, it's okay to look more like an Olympic weightlifter than a pole-vaulter. Your business IS what it processes!

Before we leave your business stomach alone to create more gastric juices, we need to discuss how you make the right decisions for your company. I suspect you already know this: Trust is a big part of masterful decision making. And the intuition you carry around inside your business gut helps you sense something before it actually happens. When you're in sync and listening to all the other parts of your business's body, there's a buzz, a level of energy, and it all comes together in your gut. When you're mired in a crucial meeting and your intuition tingles with knowing, you can see in your employees' eyes and by their body language whether an idea is good or bad. Learn to trust your own knowledge as well as other people's wisdom.

According to Dan Sullivan, founder of The Strategic Coach Program, you should take the things you do well and make them your competitive advantage. This is what Dan calls your core competency: "The most successful professionals focus on producing results and delegate everything else to a capable support staff. The most successful business owners ARE NOT workaholics." Because you are bound to hit what Dan calls the "ceiling of complexity" at some point while running your business, you can only do so much as the one driven person that you are. The only way to strengthen your business stomach is by delegating what you don't do well to others. These people resources you rely upon for better intuition lead to team building. No matter how much you know, you don't know everything.

And let's be clear about how your business intuition develops—there is no such thing as a lucky guess. Just like a scientist develops a hypothesis for any laboratory experiment, you are constantly using your business gut to make educated guesses. You sharpen your intuition by making the same mistake several times and by surrounding yourself with good people who can digest and process massive reams of information on your behalf. Your team is capable of making inferences as well as good decisions for you. And of course, you have systems in place for processing information quickly...

At last we'll delve into effective removal of the waste and toxins preventing you and your organization from maintaining a lean, agile business body. While the human body has no choice but to eliminate the waste products it doesn't need (unless you deliberately deny yourself bathroom visits), your business's digestive tract probably suffers from "analysis paralysis" more often than it should. Key indicators of blockage in your corporate colon include ongoing procrastination and a failure to act. This is no way to run a business. A healthy owner gets rid of waste quickly! And sometimes the waste you're holding onto isn't unnecessary information or too many meetings: it can be people.

You may not want to hear this, but employees with bad attitudes and work habits who sway others to the dark side of office politics can't be allowed to stay in your digestive tract. These are toxic people who should have been gone a while ago. It's your responsibility to remove anyone who compromises your business's health. I'm no medical professional, but I do know that if waste remains for too long in your human colon, it can possibly develop into polyps or even cancer. If you're feeling a bit uncomfortable after reading that last sentence, then I challenge you to do something about it. When you eat fried or rich foods your stomach can't handle, or you're possibly allergic to, your body does everything it can to expel them. You might throw up or have some other bad reaction afterward. Instead of suffering this consequence, be kind to your business's digestive system by implementing some preventive measures.

First, put your business on a high fiber diet to keep things moving in the right direction. In this case, I'm equating nutritional fiber to the worthwhile information that leads to good decision making and eliminates wasted time and effort. "Analysis paralysis" is worse than no decision at all! Don't become one of those people on a reality show such as *Hoarding: Buried Alive*. You shouldn't be trapped in your office because you can't give up your extensive bottle cap collection or won't recycle every magazine you've ever purchased since 1983. Think of your business as an expensive garage in need of a thorough cleaning out. There's a reason potty training is typically most successful with young toddlers when it's done quickly and at the right time, rather than being stretched out over too many months.

Next, you've got to be willing to recognize waste when you see it, admit that it's blocking your company's success, and take decisive action quickly. Don't be a leader who lets people, process, or technology mistakes linger. Yes, it takes a strong stomach to do it, but you've got to be capable of "pulling the trigger" and admitting to your mistakes. You also need to empower your people so that when they observe waste developing, they can eliminate it without fear of retaliation or job loss.

If what's holding you back is concern your own employees will no longer perceive you as the nice guy (or gal), then you've got a serious problem. Sure, you can outsource to someone like George Clooney's character in the movie *Up in the Air* and let a professional "downsizer" do the dirtiest work of all, eliminating people. Or, you can step up to your position as Owner or CEO and protect your company's health in a fair, respectful way. Just remember: If the waste in your real colon were to back up into your real stomach, you would be, to quote a famous line from Stanley Kubrick's *Full Metal Jacket*, "…in a world of shit." Keep your business digestive system nimble by keeping it clean.

Chapter Two Stories:

This time I'm starting with a positive story that should illuminate the power of a well-functioning business stomach. One of my manufacturing clients holds weekly brainstorming sessions with employees from a cross-section of departments, including a lab technician participant. During one particular ideation meeting, the lab technician said his daughter loves cosmetics that taste like candy. Until that moment, the company had been marketing its lip gloss products strictly to adults. But the lab technician introduced a completely different perspective to the "grab bag" of people attending the meeting by sharing some very insightful information.

So how did my client digest and process this outside information? The company added tempting candy-like flavors to their lip gloss line, and now this product extension accounts for 35% of their sales. I think the lab technician's daughter deserves a lifetime supply of lip gloss for helping her dad's company become a major competitor in the marketplace, don't you?

My next story shouldn't surprise you—it dips into the vast archive of "waste running amok." The CEO of one of my largest long-term clients started as a welder and worked his way up. Although he knew (oh yes, he did) he had some lazy employees he should cut loose from the company, he constantly consumed many other points of view to please his staff. He wanted to give his people a fair shot at being heard, but his inaction was creating blockage from within. Finally, he was fired by the company's Board of Directors for underperformance. His "analysis paralysis" regarding people had slowed down both transaction and delivery time, leading to financial losses.

One to two weeks after he left, the people he should have eliminated were indeed let go, based on nothing more than the lean metrics of profit/loss numbers. The company is now in turnaround mode, and my CEO client admitted afterward he should have handled his people issues before the company's digestive blockage had reached its critical moment. But his inaction cost both him and the company dearly.

Running your business shouldn't have to be a choice between the managerial style extremes of "pushover versus tyrant." It's okay to be compassionate with your people when appropriate, but you must be equally prepared to dispense tough love when not doing so compromises your company's health. If you don't hold your people accountable for their actions and decisions, you will have anarchy, and it will take more than an over-the-counter antacid to soothe your upset stomach. Take charge of your company's digestive health!

Chapter Three: The Optical System (Vision)

Here's a quote that may or may not be familiar to you: "The most pathetic person in the world is someone who has sight, but has no vision." Can you guess who uttered these profound words? It was Helen Keller, and I admire her all the more for having said them. Think about it. You have so many resources available to you with which to improve your physical sight: glasses, contact lenses, sunglasses, bifocals, LASIK eye surgery, and so on. But having the gift of sight doesn't mean you have VISION, especially when we talk about your company's health.

In the business world, I equate vision with focus. Your business vision should allow you to safeguard your company's future. What I mean is: It's important for you to preserve the things that are good and get rid of what's not good. You should always be asking yourself how your business's current reality fits into the future. If your vision isn't focused on the future, you need more than glasses—you need a visit to Dr. Brad's office. (And fortunately, I'm always accepting new patients…)

If you already have a "Big Hairy Audacious Goal" (from the book *Built to Last: Successful Habits of Visionary Companies*, Jim Collins & Jerry Porras) scribbled down somewhere in your office, that's a good start. Now it's time to develop clarity and wrap some intentional purpose around your goal so it will become the future. When Steve Jobs convinced Steve Wozniak to co-found Apple Computer Inc., somewhere in the garage mecca of Mountain View, California, he always knew where he wanted to get to with the company. Steve Jobs was a man with both sight and vision. Perhaps it's true he couldn't foresee all the changes he would encounter by way of my People-Process-Technology triangle. But the one thing that kept driving him (from the Apple II Macintosh, all the way to the iPod, iPhone, and iPad) was his vision. Your ability to have vision should be no different, regardless of your company's size or number of locations—it's your ultimate road map.

Your vision is where you want to end up, so you have to propel yourself and your business toward it. If you need a push in confronting your future, try this quick visualization tip from Dan Sullivan of The Strategic Coach: "If I were sitting here three years from today, looking back on today, what would have to have happened in that time for me to be happy with my progress?" In other words, paint yourself a picture of what your business's future looks like. Don't hesitate to do this. Knowing where your future lies is important to what's happening within your company right now.

Without vision, you're stuck in neutral (not so good if you're driving an automatic transmission) and most likely, you're a reactive leader. When you have vision, you're always prepared for the small skirmishes and big battles of business. Remember General Norman Schwarzkopf, Jr., (aka Stormin' Norman) of 1991 Persian Gulf War fame? He's the one who planned and led Operation Desert Storm, and booted Saddam Hussein out of Kuwait. It's been called by some historians "one of the most successful campaigns in U.S. military history." How did this leader accomplish such a thing? One word: vision. But he didn't fulfill his vision out in the shifting sands of the Middle East all by himself…

You can be capable of developing and maintaining a business vision, but without other people buying into your vision, you might as well be swimming alone, upstream. Don't fight the water and flail your arms around, wasting precious energy. Use a Total Immersion Swimming (TIS) approach (originated by swimming coach Terry Laughlin) when it comes to persuading others to grasp your business vision. With the TIS method, you become a graceful fish, swimming in your company's ocean (or very large aquarium). You glide smoothly by flicking your tail. You're quick. You conserve energy by focusing on your balance and a streamlined approach in the water. You navigate fluidly enough so that employees, clients, and supplier partners will learn to swim into the future of your vision right along with you. Just don't forget to keep your hips near the surface of the water (to reduce drag and your chances of drowning)!

Microsoft is a company that used to practice TIS when Bill Gates was the big fish leading the rest of the guppies in the tank. But when he left the company in 2008 to focus on his philanthropic efforts with the Bill & Melinda Gates Foundation, what happened to Microsoft? The company's vision went bad, and everything got blurry with the rise of mobile and smart-device technology. But this isn't what happened over at a certain Silicon Valley company named after a piece of fruit.

Yes, we're back to Steve Jobs again, a man who truly fostered and shared his business vision. (For a great read, try Walter Isaacson's biography of Steve Jobs.) He knew a CEO must ensure that the people surrounding him are capable of seeing the company's future, or success will not be reached. When Steve Jobs hired employees at Apple, he was seeking out people who would absorb and grasp his vision willingly. He believed in his quest of untethering (desktop and laptop) computers from outlets and extension cords as the future of information technology's hardware. He convinced enough people to buy into his ferocious drive for the perfect blend of entertainment and data. Apple's handheld devices are so intuitive that children and teens learn to use them faster than adults.

Think about how many industries Steve Jobs and his loyal (but oftentimes frustrated) employees revolutionized with the swipe of a finger: personal computers, animated films, music, phones, tablet computing, and digital publishing. All of this was accomplished through an intense focus on the end goal and a perfectionist obsession with rounded edges for iPhones and iPads. Your particular vision will provide guidance on what will change and what will never change within your business. Nurture it and share it with your people!

Now that we've established the need for business vision, we should discuss what type of vision you actually have. Are you myopic or hyperopic? If you see better up close than you can at far distances, then you're myopic, or nearsighted. If you see things better that are far away than you can up close, you're hyperopic, or farsighted. If you're not sure which type of vision you have, it's time for a check-up. What the heck does this have to do with business vision? Quite a bit, as you'll see.

Your core ideology and type of vision are what keep your business going, even as people leave and technology or processes evolve. (There is no escaping my PPT triangle, the three-pointed change you can count on for as long as you run your company.) As your vision is one of your business's anchors, it's important to keep checking and monitoring it, especially as your company's life cycle matures.

If your business vision is too myopic because it doesn't go beyond the four walls encasing your desk and computer configuration, the overall health of your company is in trouble. Remember the cartoon show *Mr. Magoo* from the 1960s? He was always getting into misadventures and almost-fatal situations because of what? Because of his nearsightedness, amplified by his stubborn refusal to admit he couldn't see what was in front of him!

Mr. Magoo was the luckiest of cartoon characters, though, as things would work out before the end of each episode. But he always left behind him a trail of animated destruction and chaos. The tell-tale sign of his poor vision was revealed each time he said, "Oh Magoo, you've done it again!" Don't be a Mr. Magoo when it comes to your business vision. Perhaps it's time to schedule an appointment with your friendly business optometrist, Dr. Brad. If all you need is a prescription for new glasses, consider yourself fortunate. There are many other things that can go wrong with your business vision besides nearsightedness.

I don't know when you last visited an eye doctor's office. While I don't want to scare you, I do want to jump-start your business brain into realizing just how important it is to take good care of your future goals. Beware of developing cataracts in your once-clear business vision. When the lenses inside your eyes start becoming cloudy, that means light isn't passing through easily, and your vision is getting blurry. This condition is usually age related, so the longer your business thrives, the more often you must check and adjust your vision for the future. If necessary, consider a nonsurgical intervention to remove the cloudiness. Otherwise, you will have a hard time reading your business's road map.

I fervently hope you never have to deal with a detached retina. If part, or all, of the retina peels away from the back of your eye, it will no longer work correctly. This problem can cause blurred and even loss of vision. In other words, you are in need of immediate medical attention. Imagine your business suffering a detached retina and losing vision altogether. Actually, don't imagine it—prevent it from happening at all with regular check-ups!

Yet another condition that damages business vision as a company ages is macular degeneration. That last word alone should be enough to propel you into action, I hope. In the physical world, macular degeneration is the leading cause of severe vision loss in people over age 60. Basically, the small central part of your retina (the macular) deteriorates. The risk factors for this situation include smoking, high blood pressure, obesity, being a light-skinned female, and light eye color. So that you family business owners won't feel left out, I found out that macular degeneration is possibly hereditary. The take-home lesson is this: Don't leave your vision statement trapped in an archived e-mail or PowerPoint presentation, never to be seen or revisited again. The multiple variables that can impact business vision are usually in a constant state of motion. (Don't worry—I'm not dragging you into a physics lesson here.). This is why you must ensure that your core values keep your company tethered to reality.

Additionally, by maintaining good business vision, you ensure a strong optic nerve. This is the bundle of tissue transmitting all the messages (signals) generated by your eyes to your brain. Think of the optic nerve as the communicative conduit between your company's future and your business brain. Now do you realize how important it is to take good care of your vision? Without the optic nerve, you'd never be able to communicate what you "see" to the rest of the people in your company. But there's more to business vision than just what is right in front of your eyes. You also need to pay attention to what's happening off to the side.

Your prescription glasses will help you just fine with direct vision, but you are also responsible for the good health of your peripheral vision. This is the part of your vision that occurs outside the very center of your gaze. Something to know about peripheral vision is that it's quite good at detecting motion, but not so good at distinguishing colors and shapes. Detecting motion is a critical leadership skill. Do you plan to keep your company moving toward its future goals? Your customers, competitors, and the marketplace will assuredly vacillate. You need to assess whether or not your business vision will hold steady against such changes.

If you're paying attention, peripheral vision allows you to make short-term changes to your Big Hairy Audacious Goal. Unfortunately for many CEOs and business owners, their peripheral vision is the very thing they ARE NOT noticing! It's just like being hyper-focused on traffic when you're driving somewhere, and you're desperate for a Starbucks Espresso Macchiato (FYI: only ten calories). All of a sudden, the far corner of your eye captures an image of the exact coffee mecca you seek. If this peripheral vision registers to your brain, you hightail it from the bumper-to-bumper madness and pull into the approaching Starbucks parking lot. If you ignore it, no coffee for you (and you're still stuck in commuter purgatory)...

This aspect of business vision pushes the opposite of my big, red Staples button (because it's anything BUT easy) when I'm working with clients. Your peripheral vision provides you with clues regarding what's out there that can potentially impact your business. But you have to make an effort to acknowledge and process these quick-moving prompts. The worst thing that you can do as a leader is ignore the gift of peripheral business vision and allow your blind spots to grow. Blind spots are bad. Blind spots cause unnecessary car accidents (and spilt coffee). They also cause unnecessary mistakes for your company, like not allocating your investment dollars in the right product or service at the right time or allowing a competitor to sneak ahead of you with a new product.

When working with my clients, I've noticed a direct correlation between leaders who have the best range of vision and strategic agility. If you care about your business, don't be a plow horse plodding docilely up and down the rows of a field with blinders on. Blinders just narrow your focus and create tunnel vision. How will looking at life through a kaleidoscope's pinhole allow you to thrive as a leader and grow your company? The colors are sure pretty, but you'll never see past them. And by the way, there's another crucial element that strengthens your peripheral vision, and it's not Starbucks coffee—it's your people.

Learn from Steve Jobs and hire employees who support and buy into your *Vision Quest*. (It's a movie from 1985 about a high-school wrestler. He drops two weight classes to take on a three-time state champion who's never been defeated. Talk about vision! Go ahead, Google or Bing it.) These folks will be the ones to notice the smaller details outside your direct line of vision. And by trusting your employees to use their peripheral vision well, you inherently strengthen your own ability to "see" between the lines. Your people are your collective sanity check for determining if something makes sense for the company. Glasses are helpful for correcting regular vision, but to protect your business's peripheral vision, safety goggles are a must. There's a reason they wrap around the sides of your head. You wouldn't leave them off when conducting a chemistry experiment or crafting something in a woodworking or metalworking shop, would you? Protect your peripheral vision and you ensure your company's ability to move quickly and nimbly when your business goal requires short-term adjustments.

One other aspect of business vision we haven't yet discussed is having the ability to close your eyes and look at yourself from within. A big part of vision is self-reflection. You have to be willing to admit you've made mistakes. (You should also be willing to fix any recurring mistakes.) It's almost like seeing a mirage of oasis-beckoning water in the desert after you've been out there for an hour or two or seven. Is your reflection real, or is it just something you imagine? Don't be like Narcissus, that shallow hunter from Greek mythology who fell in love with his own reflection in a pool of water. (He died from unrequited love.) Be capable and willing to adjust your vision by looking inside yourself.

Healthy CEOs or business owners must also ensure they have enough resources to fulfill their vision. It's great to close your eyes and see the picture of what will be in 20 years. It's similar to starting out in life unencumbered by responsibilities and being able to envision your dream house of the future. Isn't it always easier to see what you really want when you're closed off from outside distractions? But you have to do more than dream. Take that picture, put it on the wall, and frame it if you want to. Keep looking at your picture and working toward it until your vision becomes reality. If you're not artistic, cut out or print pretty pictures of your Big Hairy Audacious Goal and paste them onto paper to create a personal vision board. Then rally everyone necessary for successful goal fulfillment around you and your vision.

The biggest problem facing many start-ups (and more than a few longtime businesses) is that their leaders write a vision statement but never look at it again. Stop doing this! Fix this huge mistake now, and I promise I won't chastise you about it again. (That is, unless you want me to keep nudging you. I'm an excellent nudger.) Whether you call it your mission, purpose, or vision, this goal of yours is important to the various people in your business's PPT triangle. If investors don't buy into your vision, they won't give you money. If your vendors don't believe in your vision, they won't supply the right products. If your customers don't think your mission is genuine, they won't buy whatever you're selling. And if your own employees don't support your vision and adopt it as their own, they will LEAVE. This is your business vision wake-up call. Don't hit the snooze button!

You've probably had enough of the good doctor's advice regarding vision, but I'll say it again: The most important thing is to pay attention to it. If you need glasses for better use of your business vision, then wear them, because that "WYSIWYG" thing is true. What you see IS what you get. Keep your eyes open and be witness to how your business evolves. By turning away from your vision and allowing those dreaded blind spots to multiply, I guarantee you will hit the invisible wall of no-depth perception. This won't hurt you physically, but it sure will wreak havoc with your company's success.

You should review your professional vision statement quarterly, the same way you review your gross and net numbers. Include other pairs of eyes around you in this vision review process. If a people, process, or technology change is in line with your vision, do it. If a pending adjustment within your PPT triangle isn't in line with your vision, don't do it. Whatever you do, keep your business vision in focus and healthy!

Chapter Three Story:

Before I tell you a story, I'll preface it by talking a bit about the creative side of leadership. Understanding the marketplace's everyday wants and needs is what makes your vision successful. And when I say marketplace, I really mean people: customers and potential customers. Developing and fulfilling a distinct business vision takes more than intelligence—it requires imagination.

For example, the CEO of Zappo's, Tony Hsieh, doesn't view the company as a seller of merchandise. He believes Zappo's is "a service company that just happens to sell shoes." That's why his company is all about "delivering happiness." Or look at Jeff Bezos's vision statement for the almighty Amazon: "Our vision is to be the earth's most customer-centric company; to build a place where people can come to find and discover anything they might want to buy online." I think the key phrases driving Mr. Bezos's vision are "the earth's" and "find and discover anything." And in three clicks on that website, you're done helping Amazon fulfill its mission! These are creative, vision-forward leaders. But no one was, or ever will be, as capable of "Imagineering" (imagination plus engineering) as the (never cryogenically suspended) man himself, Walter Elias Disney.

According to a biography I bought at Disney World many years ago, Walt Disney started out as a humble, poor cartoonist in the 1920s. But his true ambition was to make movies. His filmmaking empire accelerated in 1928 with a black and white "talkie" short, Steamboat Willie, starring a certain stick-figure mouse named Mickey. But that's not how Uncle Walt's vision for Disneyland (and later, Disney World) came into focus. Here's how his imagination kicked in: While living in Los Angeles, California, Walt would take his young daughters, Diane and Sharon, to the carousel at Griffith Park on Sundays. He sat on the park benches with the other parents, who didn't look like they were having all that much fun. So Disney decided to create his own park-like destination that would ensure fun for the whole family. His unsatisfactory trips to a local L.A. park launched the ultimate little-and-big-kid mecca in 1955: Disneyland in Anaheim, California.

But after creating Disneyland, all the "honky-tonk" motels, retail stores, and restaurants surrounding his new destination crossed into Walt's peripheral vision. He didn't like what he saw—he knew he had to change his vision and get it right the next time. And so, when scouting locations in Florida for the birthing place of Disney World, Walt purchased all the land surrounding what would become the Magic Kingdom's structural home in 1971. Despite Uncle Walt's death in 1966, his ability to envision the future of his next theme park left plenty of room for development:

countless on-site hotel resorts, EPCOT (Experimental Prototype Community of Tomorrow), Disney's Hollywood Studios, Disney's Animal Kingdom, and two water parks. Good thing Walt's brother Roy also bought into the "Disney vision."

And remember, Walt Disney didn't start out a wealthy man. When he was a young cartoonist, no one would give him a chance. Before striking kiddie gold with Mickey Mouse (original name: Mortimer Mouse!) and those perky Mouseketeers, many of Walt's friends just about gave up on him. Even his family began to think he was crazy. But Walt Disney's vision was clear and unshakable. He was the one who was able to convince outside people to invest more money in his floundering film production company, even though his brother Roy was the money guy.

The concept of "Imagineering" was first popularized by aluminum manufacturer Alcoa in the 1940s, but Disney adopted it as his own creative process. Because of Mr. Disney's ability to stay ahead of the entertainment curve, The Walt Disney Company lives on quite successfully. And the organization's leadership will never stop pursuing continuous improvement that makes people happy. Not too shabby a visionary accomplishment, for a lousy visit to the park. I hope your business vision leads you to a "most magical place on earth": your successful company!

Chapter Four: The Auditory System (Ears/Hearing/Listening)

There is a classic rhythm and blues song that's been covered by many recording artists, from Fats Domino to Dave Edmunds (of Rockpile fame), and the chorus goes something like this: "I hear you knockin', but you can't come in…" Although the song is about a personal relationship gone sour, it might as well be about your relationship with an employee whom you refuse to listen to. We'll get to this crucial point in a little bit, because hearing is not listening. If you're not properly using those two auditory openings surrounding your business brain, don't expect your business to ever achieve optimal health.

Hearing is a key sense in more ways than you realize. Your ears allow you to detect sounds by sending vibrations traveling through the air to your middle ear and then your ear drum, causing more vibrations. Your ear drum then stimulates the three tiniest bones in your entire body: the hammer, anvil, and stirrup. (I'm starting to think a blacksmith was responsible for naming these bones.) The vibrations move along to the cochlea, a coiled tube residing within your inner ear, filled with fluid. And what happens then? These stimuli you think of as sounds turn into messages that are sent to your brain by way of the auditory nerve. Your sense of hearing also helps you maintain your balance and equilibrium. (Those of you who have ever experienced the spinning sensation of vertigo know just how debilitating an inner-ear problem can be.) But if you can't hear, then you can't listen. And if you can't listen, think about what you miss as you try to manage a successful business.

Listening is your most fundamental business fitness tool because it keeps you in tune (nope, not a joke) with your work environment and all the people populating it. It's good to know what customers and suppliers are thinking and saying about you and your company, but it's even more important to listen to the people you work with every day: your employees. The key benefit of listening to your people is that it motivates them more than the tangible rewards of a pay raise or promotion. If you don't hear what's going on with your employees and don't process those "good vibrations" (yep, that was a sly reference to the Beach Boys), you will lose your most talented people. Employees are the most valuable asset you will ever cultivate, and yet so many business owners and CEOs neglect them and disregard what they have to say. Remember my People-Process-Technology triangle? If you can't successfully nurture the people element through quality listening, the process and technology angles really don't matter. Authentic listening skills lead to learning, which leads to better decisions and a more strategic direction. Because when the hand goes up, your mouth should go shut (or something like that)!

That's right—listening is the most important part of communicating with another human being who happens to work for you. When I begin working with a client, I spend most of my time listening. This is how I learn about the pain causing a problem or conflict within the company. I need to listen first before jumping in with my consulting voice so I can accurately identify the problem and make it go away. I also listen to what isn't being said or mentioned, so I can ask intelligent questions about these missing-in-action gaps. Any successful salesperson will tell you that the most important part of the selling process is: knowing when to "stifle it" and listen.

When you demonstrate to your employees that you're capable of listening to them, you simultaneously encourage them to become good listeners. What people love most about you as a boss is that you listen to them. What better way is there to demonstrate you value the profitable thoughts brewing inside an employee's business brain? A healthy communicative process starts with good listening. Unfortunately, too many of you are only hearing the words that escape from your employees' mouths...

According to a 2010 article by Bob Moulsong of the *Times of Northwest Indiana*, "Hearing is the physical ability, while listening is a skill. Listening allows one to make sense of and understand what another person is saying... the meaning behind the words." From my perspective, one is active (listening), and one is passive (hearing). Your business brain is engaged and processing actionable information when you listen. If all you're doing is hearing vowels and syllables without thinking about them, your brain is merely on autopilot and accepting the information at face value.

Why should you be concerned with the difference between hearing and listening? I'll tell you why: Without healthy listening skills, you risk the chance of permanently disabling the people aspect of your company's PPT triangle. If you constantly tune out by only hearing, you have no idea what's really going on within your company. The new tagline or slogan for your business might as well be "The Sound of Silence," that is if songwriter Paul Simon would be gracious enough not to charge you a royalty fee. The benefits of listening are enormous. Listening is the critical difference between knowing when your people are making statements versus asking questions.

By being an active listener, you gain so much in terms of employee trust. When the people working for you believe you are actually listening to what they say and making appropriate decisions based on that information, your credibility as a problem solver deepens. By listening, you develop solutions and remove conflict. An active listener makes a conscious effort to break through obligatory hearing and understand the complete message. When you listen actively for comprehension, it impacts people's perceptions of you as a leader. Your better listening habits should lead to taking action, which then leads to conflict resolution.

This may sound obvious, but by understanding others better, it helps them understand you. You learn by listening. You foster rapport, trust, professional intimacy, and personal motivation by listening to your employees. The profile of an excellent listener is someone who blocks out distractions during a conversation, doesn't form counterarguments while the other person is speaking, and demonstrates engagement with positive verbal cues, eye contact, and body language. But I never said this would be easy. A *New York Times* article I intermittently reread from November

2012 ("Why Listening Is So Much More Than Hearing") says it all: "Hearing, in short, is easy... Listening is a skill that we're in danger of losing in a world of digital distraction and information overload." Let's get you past the danger point by talking about concrete ways to listen more effectively to your people.

First, you might need to remove any excess wax buildup in your business listening apparatus. I'm half joking and half not joking. The earwax produced by your ear canal helps in many ways. It cleans and lubricates your ear canal and also provides some protection from outside bacteria and water. But too much (or impacted) earwax can press against your ear drum, causing a blocked external auditory canal and hearing loss. The American Academy of Otolaryngology discourages removal of earwax unless it's causing you a serious health problem.

But here's the thing about removing earwax when it's absolutely necessary—you should never use a cotton swab. This will just push the wax further into your ear canal, and you could perforate your ear drum. My advice is to throw out those Q-tips® and make an appointment with a medical doctor! If all that's in your ears right now are ear plugs instead of too much earwax, take them out and get ready to change how you engage with your people and collect information from them.

You should maintain an open-door policy encouraging your employees to speak up rather than shut up. You should also plan intermittent "focus group" discussions with your company's staff and workers. Yes, you will need to make time for this listening research, but don't dismiss it as unnecessary. At a previous employer way back when, I used to run "Bagels and Bytes" sessions. We would invite customers to our corporate office and ask them face-to-face for honest feedback about our services. If you do something like this with your employees, you'll be amazed by what you learn in an hour or two. The whole purpose of listening is to gather actionable information. If you give any of these techniques a try, you will gain, and I'm not talking about weight.

Once you've got your people together in a room, ask probing questions, and don't be afraid of drilling down to uncover the root cause of a troubling issue. Another good use of this listening time is to solicit feedback regarding ways to expand your company's product line or service offerings. If you suspect your people won't be completely honest in your presence, your backup plan is as simple as installing a feedback/suggestion box. Just be sure to actually read through your employees' suggestions on a regular basis (at least weekly). Whether by open door, focus group meeting or suggestion box, you'll demonstrate you're not a myopic leader hiding in his or her office, waiting for things to get better on their own.

Let your people know they are heard. Allow them to offer suggestions and solutions. And then watch their motivation and vested interest in your business surge. This is how you amplify your listening skills without buying an expensive hearing aid. In the movie *This Is Spinal Tap*, there's a great scene between Nigel Tufnel (the band's guitarist) and Marty DiBergi (the fictional film director making a *Spinal Tap* documentary) regarding the fact that the numbers on Nigel's amplifier "all go to eleven." I don't want to screw it up, so here's the exact quote: "Well, it's one louder, isn't it? It's not ten. You see, most blokes, you know, will be playing at ten. You're on ten here, all the way up, all the way up, all the way up, you're on ten on your guitar. Where can you go from there? Where?" Don't hesitate to let your business amplifier go all the way to eleven!

Would you rather have too much or not enough information when it comes to your company's success (or failure)? Venture beyond your inner sanctum and gather opinions, likes, dislikes, and insights from the people who should be your most enthusiastic cheerleaders: your employees. If big-brand companies can use marketing research to generate successive hits in the consumer world, you can use this listening tool to make your company healthier from within.

Here's an example of why listening is so crucial to your business's health. The Coca-Cola Company conducts excellent consumer research, some of which involves using a model convenience store specifically designed to capture participant's shopping behavior. But Coca Cola learned a harsh listening lesson back in 1985 (despite initial taste-testing results) that prevented utter catastrophe.

Do you remember a little blip on the consumer radar screen called New Coke? This reformulated beverage was introduced on April 23, 1985 to replace Coke's original formula. First known as "the new taste of Coca-Cola" (and much later on as

Coca-Cola II in 1992), New Coke was a marketing disaster that elicited hatred in the hearts of loyal Coke fanatics. Although the secret research (code name: Project Kansas) conducted to test and perfect New Coke's flavor was mostly positive, a small (and incredibly vocal) minority of focus group participants made it clear they just might stop drinking Coke, period. That's how angry it made them to find out the Coca-Cola Company would consider replacing their beloved Coke with a different formula.

Once New Coke was formally introduced, the focus-group results played out similarly in the real world. The company received an avalanche of phone calls and letters that seemingly implied consumers felt they were losing a beloved family member! The reality was that the vocal minority was more upset about losing access to Coke's old/classic formula than the taste of the new formula. And so, Coca-Cola executives announced the return of the original formula (aka Coca-Cola Classic, aka Coke Classic, aka Old Coke) on July 10, 1985. Long live active listening and Coca-Cola's ability to admit they had made a big mistake.

For optimal listening research both internally and externally, be willing to take on as many different approaches that help answer the ultimate business question of "Why?" Informal surveys, online and print questionnaires, post-purchase and customer satisfaction surveys, focus groups, one-on-ones, secret or mystery shoppers—all are ways to follow up and find out why you lost a good client/account or a pending sale. Listening is the means by which you'll find out what works and what doesn't work in your company.

And by the way: If it just so happens that YOU are the problem in need of resolution, ask an objective third party or intermediary to do the listening for you. When everyone is afraid of "the boss," your key HR person could be the "ear of reason" you need most. Never rule out indirect listening if it produces actionable results, but be advised to become a better/active listener (so your people will view you as approachable).

So far we've talked about using your business hearing to listen to the voices in the physical world. Given the online tidal wave (the Internet, e-mail, social media) that has permanently hijacked us all, it's important you learn how to listen to and process this inbound information. I know it can seem overwhelming, but it doesn't have to be. That's because you don't need to listen to all of it! The key to online listening is determining which streams of information are relevant to pushing your company and your people forward. Yes, this is a growing aspect of your PPT triangle's technology angle, and it's not going away anytime soon. Learn how to listen well with your computer monitor and keyboard or mobile smart device, but don't develop tinnitus. You know, that ringing in the ears, the sensation of hearing a buzzing, hissing, chirping or other sound which can lead to partial hearing loss. Prolonged exposure to loud sounds is the most common cause of tinnitus. You must master the art of online listening to ward off "virtual" tinnitus.

One simple way to winnow down the avalanche of online information vying for your attention is by setting up alerts as your online listening stations. As I mentioned in Chapter One, you can create Google Alerts (via your Google account) that search for stories and articles related to your industry's keywords and important trends. You determine whether you want the Google Alert e-mails delivered in real time, daily, or weekly. I suggest starting out slow so you don't become an indentured servant to your inbox. Another listening tool available to you is subscribing to a website's RSS feed (Really Simple Syndication). This is an easy way to collect and process headlines and updated information from online sources relevant to your industry without having to spend additional time hunting it down.

Another healthy online listening habit is setting up accounts with various online software/websites that allow you to measure your company's social influence on others and manage your digital brand. Klout is an online app that uses social media platforms and analytics to rank its users' online social influence with a Klout score (of 0 – 100). Klout lets you know what your specific areas of influence are based on the content you post and curate online. HootSuite is a website and online brand management service with which you can publish online content to many social media accounts. The HootSuite dashboard becomes your listening control center. Another useful social media platform for online brand management is SproutSocial. This site also offers analytics/demographics and a high-level dashboard for monitoring how your online friends and followers are reacting to your social media activity, but there is a monthly fee. Right now, I happen to think SproutSocial is a great way for small businesses to monitor their online social influence.

One other tool that amplifies digital listening within your company is Yammer. It's a freemium enterprise social network service used for private, intra-organizational communication. Once you set up Yammer for your business, employees join the company's Yammer network and "talk" with each other. In order to benefit from any of these measurement tools, you do need to be active on several of social media's usual suspects: Facebook, Twitter, LinkedIn, Pinterest, Foursquare, Google+, Instagram, YouTube, and so on. And there are a million ways to listen online: status updates, posts, tweets, pins, etc. A side benefit of social media activity is that when you access the online information of people you know, it gets pulled into your in-house CRM (Customer Relationship Management) software and xRM (Anything Relationship Management) data.

You can also filter and brand what's important to you and your followers/connections by including hashtags in your social media posts. A hashtag is a word or phrase with a pound sign in front of it (such as #BizFitRevolution) that functions as a keyword search. If you're not listening online and engaging with the folks you're listening to, I guarantee your competitors are, so don't ignore the sounds of social media. All this listening will help you become a better marketer.

Another thing to know about online listening is that e-mail is not facing its untimely demise just yet. You need to keep your inbox healthy and junk-free. When viewing your e-mail inbox, scan the subject lines for keywords of interest. Get yourself into the habit of going through your inbox quickly. If an e-mail is actionable and you need to do something about it, keep it. If an e-mail is a potential "time suck" and not actionable, delete it without regret. Do yourself a favor and set up routing instructions for a "To Be Read" file within your e-mail software. Mail routing and delivery options are available in most e-mail services such as Google Gmail, Hotmail, Outlook, etc. If you're not sure how to do this, have your IT person explain it or set it up for you.

You can learn a lot from e-mail, but since vocal intonation isn't communicated with words on a screen, you can't detect someone's real emotion. (Unless the Caps Lock is on while typing—this is the universally understood version of yelling online. Here's my advice about communicating by e-mail in all caps: Don't do it.)

When you're on the receiving end of an e-mail causing your blood pressure to skyrocket, don't react by sending an angry reply. Just walk away from your desk (or put down your mobile device) and breathe while you cool down. If you're caught up in an important e-mail exchange and you can't clarify your message within three e-mails, pick up the phone and communicate the old-fashioned way. Whether you're communicating positive or negative information in an e-mail exchange, it always requires some element of clarification. Constant communication by e-mail can make you tone deaf. You lose the ability to pick up on the other person's emotional cues. In general, e-mail is an unhealthy way to "listen" all the time. (Your verbal tone is important to successful communication; we'll discuss tone in detail in the Vocal Cords/Voice chapter.)

So, never make any assumptions about an e-mail you absolutely must send. Ask questions and investigate further, assess what your motivation is and what caused you to send that particular e-mail. Again, e-mail itself as a communicative conduit has deadened your sense of listening and altered your processing abilities. Because e-mail fosters a bit of tone deafness in all of us, you have to figure out an e-mail message's intent and true emotion. A good analogy is that well-known AAMCO commercial forever circulating online (thanks to YouTube). It's the one in which a variety of actors mimic how their cars sound because they can't express the problem with words. Then the nice, patient AAMCO mechanic smiles and says, "We can fix that." Just so you know, AAMCO's ad agency dubbed this the "We Hear You" campaign. If you can't figure out the "sounds" you need to make or interpret through e-mail, it's time for some phone or face-to-face listening.

As a professional listener, I don't believe there's any difference between how you listen internally to the people who work for you versus listening to all the players external to your company. But I do think you have to address the differing sets of information hitting your eardrums and distinguish among the various points of view regarding your business. I would also suggest you be more empathetic to your employees' voices, but not reveal as much of a "soft spot" to your customers and clients. When interacting with your workers, each conversation is an opportunity to nurture professional intimacy, which increases personal motivation. But your active listening just doesn't go as deep with a customer, so you may want to keep it less personal. (You can still make a positive connection regarding your products or services, trust me.) When you work with someone daily and face many business decisions and dilemmas together, it's best to build trust by giving them your full listening attention. Selective listening is not an option!

Before we get to this chapter's story, I will gently remind you that active listening is the single most important skill you possess as a business owner. A healthy auditory system dictates how well you do in the marketplace. Proper listening answers all the questions. That's what your business is all about—getting answers that improve the processes running parallel to your questions. Internally, how do you know who has what talent or skillset within your company unless you listen? Optimized listening diffuses anger, breaks down barriers, makes your work environment a happier place, and transforms you into a more collaborative leader. The truth is as simple as this: The more you sincerely listen to your employees, the more you'll be spoken to by them. Also, active listening can't help but improve your external relationships with customers and suppliers and keep you at the top of someone's "call list."

Don't ever push the mute button on your company's remote control unless you deem listening a waste of your time. In the classic Dr. Seuss book *Horton Hears a Who*, that small speck of dust, which no one else but Horton the Elephant could hear (initially), turned out to be an entire, populated planet. Good thing Horton didn't let the other animals living in his jungle destroy the kind citizens of Whoville by boiling them in "Beezle-Nut" oil! Just remember: "A person's a person, no matter how small," so acknowledge your employees' existence in the best way possible and LISTEN.

Chapter Four Story:

I have a software-developer client whose leadership asked me to create business and marketing plans that would grow their sales organization and revenue. Since the company has regional opportunities on the East Coast, this was good thinking by my client. Since they are paying me, I submitted the requested plans to them not once, but twice. And what I got in return was: crickets (as in no reply).

Because I never get a response or any feedback from my senior management contacts, I end up speaking with staff employees when I'm on-site. And guess what I found out by listening to the people handling the company's day-to-day work? I learned that the company's employees never receive announcements or communication regarding important decisions and new hires. I also know these folks are obscenely underpaid and unhappy. Their suggestions are (consistently) ignored by their bosses. Additionally, this client's personnel turnover is much higher than that of their industry's competitors. I've put an actionable plan in front of them, but they still don't understand why their sales numbers aren't growing.

Finally, I got to the root cause of this client's dilemma. Their problem isn't really sales—it's the ability to close a sale during the proposal process. They ask themselves the same questions over and over again, but they never submit new or innovative answers in response to an RFP. The proposal process takes them twice as long as it should. Just like what happens at the end of Hans Christian Andersen's fairy tale "The Emperor's New Clothes," my client's top leaders don't think they're walking the floors naked. Change isn't happening because they aren't listening to me. Even worse, they aren't listening to their own people.

Organizational dysfunctionality will continue to drag this client down for as long as senior management remains too busy to listen actively and take action. They hide behind tone-deaf e-mails communicating nothing, and they are doomed to repeat this critical mistake "to infinity and beyond." I could pull a classic Jack Palance move (from the 1991 Academy Awards ceremony) and get their attention with some one-armed push-ups, but even that wouldn't restore their unfortunate hearing loss. Sadly, not all my stories end well…

Chapter Five: The Vocal Cords/Resonator System (Voice)

As an entrepreneur, your voice provides you with the ability to express your company's unique message or core differentiator. The words that come out of your mouth should be a beacon in the darkness and an outer reflection of your inner company. In other words, your business voice is who you are. And you share it constantly with all the people connected to you professionally: employees, customers, suppliers, and even competitors. Your voice should be in line with your company's Big Hairy Audacious Goal, and most important, it should convey information clearly and consistently. But in the fast-moving business world, we all know that message sent doesn't always equal message received. This is why you need to start paying attention to the nuances of your business voice, both verbally and nonverbally.

One main reason verbal communication short-circuits is that too many times, your people are on the receiving end of mixed messages. The information being said by you may be factually correct, but the sounds vibrating within your vocal cords (which are actually membrane folds stretched across your larynx) may or may not match your message. Take a deep breath (okay, let it out) and listen to the tone and pitch of your voice. When you express yourself to others, are you yelling, or do you sound like a collaborative, approachable person? Is your vocal style full of relentless teasing that leaves your employees wondering what you really mean? Do you sound so deathly serious all the time that your verbal communication generates twitchy, neurotic behavior within your company? Your voice's "mood" is just as important as your actual words if you want people to believe what you're saying. Leaders who demonstrate a "do as I say, not as I do" verbal style are going to butt their heads against the wall of credibility, but hard. And trust me, it's going to hurt.

In *Full Metal Jacket*, Stanley Kubrick's classic film about the Vietnam War, a hard-core killing machine known as Animal Mother says the following to the film's main character, Private Joker: "You talk the talk. Do you walk the walk?" Perhaps this line is now considered cliché, but from my viewpoint as a business consultant, it's critical to your voice's message. Do you lead by example in a productive way, and do you follow your own good advice? If your employees can be heard yelling at customers or clients during phone discussions, your internal voice has transformed into a communal megaphone that should never pierce the outside world. I can't imagine the feedback you get from these unfortunate souls would tell you good, happy things.

Never forget that your business voice needs to be an accurate echo of what you want others to say about you and your company. In Greek mythology, there was a mountain nymph named Echo who was punished by Hera, the queen of the gods, for helping her amorous husband Zeus in one of his many sordid love affairs. Because Hera took away Echo's ability to speak her own thoughts and feelings, the only way poor Echo could communicate was by repeating someone's last words. If you want your voice's echo to reflect well as communication circulates outside your work environment, make sure the original message is clear and credible. One way to ensure this is to have your business brain check your outgoing messages…

Your parents said this, and I'm sure some good teachers and/or professors also told you this in your formative years, so now it's my turn to say it: The most important thing you can do to improve your communicative style is to listen before you speak. We discussed the whole "hearing versus listening" thing in the previous chapter, but now I'm asking you to listen critically to your own voice. Do you know that when you talk, your vocal cord movements are "a result of the coordinated contraction of various muscles that are controlled by the brain through a specific set of nerves?" That's right—your business brain is intimately involved in vocalization, so it makes sense to listen first by practicing what you're going to say.

For even better assurance that your message is clear, gather a few of your most trusted employees and practice in front of them. Don't be afraid to vocalize. Ask if you're getting your true message across before sharing it with outside strategic partners and your customers. I could make a really bad joke right now about how to get your business voice to Carnegie Hall, but I won't. (And by the way: Even though the punch line is strongly associated with iconic comedian Jack Benny, he didn't originate it. I thought you might want to know…)

While you're thinking and practicing to ensure no one reacts negatively to your message, don't just share it and think you've done your best. Verbal communication can be a tricky thing. The words that remain unspoken by you can be interpreted incorrectly and muddle your well-intended message. Bottom line, you need to balance your business voice in a way that hits the middle between too little information and the dreaded TMI (Too Much Information)! When you leave out the bits and pieces of information that are given assumptions to you (but not to your audience), you risk being unclear. Message length and timing are important elements in your quest for successful business communication. Perhaps you drone on for too long during a meeting. And perhaps it turns out that you convey the most important part of your message in the last few minutes (as your people tap their smartphones mindlessly or glance at the conference room's clock.). Please don't expect anyone to remember the exact thing that you want them to do. See how important it is to pay attention to your business voice and listen well?

How loudly or not you express your message is another important aspect of successful verbal communication. Maybe I'm about to date myself, but this example is so good that I don't mind. Have you ever heard of Crazy Eddie (original company name: ERS Electronics)? This discount electronics company bombarded the New York tri-state area with hard-to-forget radio and TV commercials in the 1970s and 1980s. At the end of every TV commercial, an actor representing the Crazy Eddie chain (the co-founder's real name is Eddie Antar) appeared ready to foam at the mouth and said, "His prices are INSANE!" But it wasn't just the deep-discount pricing that was off its rocker—the company's message was VOCALLY insane.

As it turns out, the U.S. Attorney's office in New Jersey opened a federal grand jury investigation in 1987 regarding Crazy Eddie's warranty billing practices. That same year, the Securities and Exchange Commission investigated alleged violations of federal securities law by some of the company's officers and employees. The company became the poster child for corporate fraud before the 1980s were over, and Eddie Antar fled the U.S. for Israel in early 1990. So the lesson is: Be careful how you intonate your message to the public!

Another communicative challenge you need to be wary of is overusing your voice. If you're "vocally insane" because your messages are accompanied by a lot of screaming or yelling, your physical voice will demoralize others. And you just might end up with a bad case of laryngitis. This inflammation of the voice box (your larynx) will cause your voice to become raspy or hoarse. While laryngitis is usually caused by a cold or the flu, all that inappropriate vocalizing to your people will definitely plague you in the form of no voice at all. If this is your verbal style at work, you need to follow Doctor Brad's home treatment: rest your voice (literally), use a humidifier or vaporizer to soothe your voice box, and drink plenty of fluids. Once you've calmed yourself down, you should think before your next attempt to communicate with anyone affiliated with your business.

Just because you've trapped yourself into a corner of bad verbal communication doesn't mean you should stop talking to your employees. I've worked with my share of CEO "screamers," but I've also been hired by business owners who could have been big stars during Hollywood's silent movie era. Sadly, nonverbal leaders make the worst mistake of all. When you're the business brain, when you're the one creating your company's vision, you should never hide behind layers of organizational communication and send tone-deaf e-mails and memos. In this case, silence IS NOT golden—it's deadly.

If you have bad news to share with a particular employee or department, people want to receive it in person, face-to-face. Whether your message is positive or negative, don't be afraid to verbalize it. CEOs and business owners lose their most talented people when perceived as leaders who don't communicate verbally. In fact, a *Forbes* article from June 2013 ("Six Reasons Your Best Employees Quit You") states this even more bluntly: "There's a saying that employees don't leave companies, they leave managers." If you continue to ignore your employees verbally, their lack of satisfaction can translate into an alarming trend of two-week notices. Please don't frustrate the people who need to hear your voice the most.

Whether you manufacture something or provide a service, get out on the floor and talk with your employees. After all, you rely upon them to internalize your business voice and share it with the outside world, don't you? Do your best to avoid any negative words or tone when you're communicating inside your company. According to Scott Adams, creator of the *Dilbert* cartoon series and books, "One 'oh shit' can erase a thousand 'attaboys.'" Instead of leading with a negative, start with the "attaboy," and have your business brain and voice collaborate more often to steer clear of the "oh shits" (especially in public). Wouldn't it be nice if more of your employees decide to stay because they're getting more "attaboys" from you? Yes, this is a rhetorical question—no need to vocalize here.

Also, be conscious of your verbal style, and measure your tone. Strive to sound calm, not high-pitched and whiney. If you're in a bad mood and your tone matches, I guarantee it will drip down to your employees. In fact, your vocal tone alone will cause your people to perceive that you're mad at them, even if your foul mood is based on something (or someone) external to the company. Whenever you talk with anyone affiliated with your business, always aim for a constructive tone. A "destructive" tone is exactly that and will leave many casualties within your business relationships.

And by the way: Not speaking with your customers and suppliers is just as bad as little-to-no verbal communication with your employees. If you're not reaching out to your customers by phone (or in person), then you really don't know what's going on out in the "street." Verbal interaction with suppliers and other strategic partners gives you access to a more objective viewpoint regarding competitive intelligence. It's so much better to ask questions about trends and news regarding your particular marketplace in a back-and-forth conversation. It can be maddening to do so all the time through e-mail or social media. Don't rely solely on passive communication with your "outside" people—these folks actually do care about your success. Pick up the damn phone regularly and have meaningful conversations. And no, text messaging via your smartphone doesn't count.

Regardless of whom you're talking to, you should discover for yourself what you sound like in conversation with others. You can accomplish this intermittently by reciting an important e-mail or other written communication out loud and recording it. When you play back the recording, pay close attention to your tone. Is it calm and positive, or angry and destructive? What is the pitch of your voice—is it high, low, or just right? And what about the rate/speed of the words coming out of your mouth—is it too fast, too slow, or nice and balanced? No matter what you're really feeling while actively communicating, your tone implies emotion, and that's something you must learn to control as a leader.

The key emotional factor to healthy verbal communication with all the different people in your professional life is consistent pitch and tone. I'll tell you something that shouldn't surprise you: All the great leaders of the world never get riled when speaking. They don't have to think about how they sound because it's ingrained within their leadership style. The way a calm, controlled communicator talks in public is exactly how he or she talks in private. If you can master a consistent pitch and tone with your vocal cords, you will transform your business voice into an instrument of communicative success.

Think about how a press secretary for the President of the United States gets behind that podium in the Briefing Room day after day to share information with and field questions from the press. Despite all the loaded (and unloaded) questions hurled at (former) incumbent Jay Carney (or predecessors such as Scott McClellan, Dee Dee Myers, and James Brady), you never see him sweat. Model your own verbal style after the press secretary of your choice for a calm and consistent business voice.

I'll give you an even more specific example sure to rile a few sports enthusiasts. If you live in the Philadelphia, PA, tri-state area, the name Jeffrey Lurie should mean something to you. For those of you who don't know, Mr. Lurie has been the owner of the Philadelphia Eagles football team since 1994. A Boston boy who attempted to buy the New England Patriots in 1993, Jeffrey Lurie is perceived by many Philadelphia-area football fanatics as a boring and droll kind of guy. But when I close my eyes and listen to his business voice, what I hear is a strong leader who communicates post-game in the same calm tone whether the Eagles win or lose.

When Coach Andy Reid was finally close enough to getting pushed off the "firing" cliff, here's what steady Jeffrey told the local media: "...I don't like situations to become sideshows. It's just not my style. I'll reflect and analyze afterwards, and that's what I've always done." You may not own a football team, but surely you encounter tough decisions (such as the firing of Andy Reid). The best way to steer your ship upright and into calmer waters is by communicating your message with a consistent, controlled voice.

A nonprofit example of a successful leader who never let external factors disturb her message of healing is the "Angel of the Battlefield" and founder of the American Red Cross, Clara Barton. Shy and timid as a child, Clara Barton found her true voice as a nurse during the Civil War. By 1864, she was appointed by a Union general as the "lady in charge" of all frontline hospitals for the Army of the James. After the war, Miss Barton travelled to Europe to help the Red Cross society during the Franco-Prussian War. Back home in the States, she began advocating for recognition of the International Committee of the Red Cross in the early 1870s. By 1881, she became President of the American Red Cross and was admired for her steady (and persistent) message of being ready to respond to human crises other than war. Need more proof of how rewarding consistency is to your business voice? At least 36 roads, schools, and other designated places (including a certain rest area on the New Jersey Turnpike) in the U.S. are named after Clara Barton. If she could be verbally consistent while bullets whizzed by her on life-threatening battlefields, so can you (on the business battlefield)!

Beyond being master of your vocal domain, you should sense by now that the best way to share information with your employees is verbally, without filler or emotion. Overwhelmed by their reality of too much e-mail and too many text messages and social media posts, your people are desperate for you to speak with them face-to-face. But when you talk out loud, stay the course and tell people what they need to hear rather than what they want to hear. What I mean is: avoid any verbal bullshit! Regardless of your actual emotions, your message should remain steady, just like Led Zeppelin's *The Song Remains the Same*.

Don't allow emotional unbalance to creep into your pitch and tone. You are the one who controls your business voice. When your tone and pitch shift due to emotion, your message can get lost. An ineffective leader can always be singled out in a group setting by his or her mixed, inconsistent message and verbal style. Before a mental analysis of your words even begins, people pick up immediately on your nonverbal messages and interpret your intent based on your voice. Consistency is your number one asset for successful verbal communication. It also helps to know your audience before unleashing your crisp, clear, and controlled message.

You know that philosophical question, "If a tree falls in the forest and no one is around to hear it, does it make a sound?" In the business world, your voice is the tree. If your message isn't appropriate for your audience, whether you're a graceful willow or a mighty redwood, no one will listen. When message sent doesn't equal message received, you need to regroup and determine the appropriate communicative process (and the right words) for the people part of your PPT triangle. Ever hear of a man named Marshall McLuhan? He was a Canadian philosopher and authentic guru of communication theory in the 1960s and 70s. He is the guy who originated "the global village" and "the medium is the message." This second famous phrase generally applies to radio, TV, print and online communication. But within a company or business, your voice is the medium, and you need to make sure your message isn't just heard but understood. In the academic world, The Uncertainty Reduction Theory states that people want certainty and predictability in their communicative relationships. The best way to achieve this is by using your voice to deliver messages that accurately target the different audiences you deal with daily.

While we're still discussing proper control of your emotions, let's finish our conversation about how to handle your negative feelings. If you're upset, you need to step away from your desk or conference room. Anger leads to a disconnect between your business brain and voice. There is no good message in anger. Once the hurtful words in your angry message slip from your lips, you can't ever take them back. As soon as you say them, you know you've done some damage. If your business brain is missing in action, put yourself in time-out. Write down what it is you want to say and read it aloud to ensure it's the right message, minus the heated emotion that could start a metaphoric brush fire throughout your company. It's hard for your business brain to think clearly when anger enters the arena—don't be a Roman emperor and verbally throw your people to the lions.

When a frustrated mother constantly yells at her young child, all she's communicating is a negative message that says "don't pay attention to my words." So the kid fulfills her wishes by tuning her out! Anger should be saved for those rare occasions when the voice of reason is absent. But resist the urge or bad habit of using it in everyday communications. Don't let your day-to-day messages get lost in volcanic eruptions of anger—maintain your business voice of reason. After all, others judge you not only by how you look but by how you sound.

That's right, I'm going to say it: First impressions are EVERYTHING, and your message is half of the equation. Again, it's not just the words coming out of your mouth. Your verbal pitch and tone, your rate of speech, your unique way of vocalizing all impact your business relationships from the very first moment you speak (whether with one person or in front of several hundred people). First impressions set the communicative tone for how you run your business. How you say what you say lets people know whether you're sincere (or a verbal politician), flexible (or rigid), approachable (or guarded by an invisible electronic fence), and so on. When there's a management change and employees know "there's a new sheriff in town," you get that one chance to make a sincere first impression. New business owners or CEOs in particular should observe and listen for a bit before entering "first-impression territory." I say this because your initial company-wide speech will reveal many things about your leadership style.

Again, your business voice is a form of verbal branding as well as your core differentiator. Be sure of what it is you want the outside world to know about your company before the message infiltrates your print and online marketing/social-media efforts. And by the way, did you know that the original title of Jane Austen's beloved book of verbal ping-pong and misunderstood messages, *Pride and Prejudice*, was originally titled *First*

Impressions" If ever you want to confirm just how much damage an unhealthy business voice can cause your company, I challenge you to read Miss Austen's novel.

Before we get to my client story, I'll give this communication thing one last spin. As your company's leader, you need to communicate verbally with employees, suppliers and customers, and you need to do it well. A unified voice and message must be supported by consistent behavior, or you'll lose all credibility with the people in your professional world. Above all, don't get caught in a lie, unless you want to be in the uncomfortable (and unhealthy) position of having to walk back your words and manage your company's reputation in crisis mode. Businesses with a sound communicative style are more profitable, reduce their transaction time, and have happier employees (and less turnover). If you communicate well, your business will be healthy. If not, your business will be unhealthy. That's it. Good communication by the top leadership is a pathway to success, so find your true business voice and practice, practice, practice (all the way to Carnegie Hall).

Chapter Five Story:

I have a client with a heating, ventilation, and air conditioning business who had a clear internal message that wasn't aligned with his company's external voice. When growth of his residential customer base plateaued, my client finally acknowledged his Big Hairy Audacious Goal. He wanted to gain more commercial market share in his state/region and become "The Contractor's Contractor" of HVAC services. Great goal, but he also had a big, hairy, audacious problem—all his marketing and promotional communication to the outside world was focused on residential services. This included advertising in that workhorse of a previous generation, the Yellow Pages. But business was dropping. And construction firms/contractors didn't perceive him or his company as having the expertise needed for commercial HVAC work.

He started using nontraditional methods (i.e., online and social media) to promote his company, but the word "residential" kept slipping from his lips. When he tried marketing to the commercial HVAC sector, the message that his target audience wanted to hear wasn't what they were told. And when his employees were told to go out and promote their services, they kept hitting residential areas, not commercial buildings. Because the company's external voice wasn't consistent with my client's aspirations, message sent was most definitely not message received. So what do you think I counseled him to do? Yep, I told him to turn up the heat on his commercial "thermostat" and set his residential voice to permanent "cooling."

Once he acknowledged the vocal disconnect, my client gargled with some warm salt water before changing his outside voice to match his inside voice. He adapted his marketing communication efforts to speak directly to the needs and wants of commercial HVAC customers, and his reality changed. The previous year, my client had a measly 5% of commercial market share in his territory. Within the first month of using his now-balanced business voice, he increased the company's commercial HVAC revenue by 35%. Because he aligned the company's marketing message with his Big Hairy Audacious Goal, business began doubling and tripling more effectively than a Trane ComfortLink™ II Zoning System. Sometimes, healing your sickly business vocal cords is as simple as that!

Chapter Six: The Cardiovascular System (Your Heartbeat, the Soul of Your Business)

I don't doubt your business is near and dear to your heart, but tell me: Do you wear your business heart on your sleeve, or do you have a business heart of stone? In today's high-tech society, consumers are generally mistrustful of what they consider cold, soulless machines of enterprise. And many "millennials" (aka Generation Y, born between the early 1980s and the early 2000s) want and seek a purpose-driven life that includes a socially responsible employer. One business practice I deem essential to your company's "heartbeat" is letting people know you have other motives beyond raking in cash. Giving back to the community in which your business dwells breeds a better corporate culture and demonstrates an ability to succeed (but not at the expense of others). I'm talking about your company's ability to create "shared value."

I'll defer now to Michael Porter, a Harvard Business School professor who's considered a leading authority on regional/global business strategy and competitiveness. Professor Porter's concept of shared value "involves creating economic value in a way that also creates value for society by addressing its needs and challenges. Businesses must reconnect company success with social progress." While he's not proposing you give away all your profits, Professor Porter is suggesting you change your mind-set regarding how and where business performance and society INTERSECT. This notion of shared value should be part of your business vision. It should influence how you interact with your employees. It's up to you to teach your people there is more to life than making money. Revenue is a necessity, but it shouldn't be your sole motivator. Please integrate this fact into your business's soul: People work harder when they're passionate about a cause or goal that transcends economic security. I say this with a lot of confidence. Capitalism as a "dog-eat-dog" way of life is shifting. Don't be naïve by convincing yourself your competitors aren't moving in this direction. They are. A healthy business needs a healthy society.

When people contemplate your company, it's preferable that they like and trust you. Whatever your primary inspiration or passion in life, let it lead your business to support human causes in your community, state, country, or world. I want you to make a profit, but I also want you to make a difference. You'll know you're doing the right thing if you follow Buddy Holly's emotional cue: "Heartbeat, why do you miss when my baby kisses me?" Your business's heart should skip from time to time whenever your personal ethics benefit both employees and external relationships.

We've come to the chapter in this book where you need to look beyond your physical appearance and stare into your soul. Leading by example sounds easy, but we all know it's a daily effort that builds upon itself. Establish yourself and your company as role models in your industry. One excellent way to begin doing this is by connecting with your immediate community. Offer your people incentives to get involved with the human ecosystem of your business's habitat. Contests, charitable collections, and volunteer activities all keep your business heart strong and healthy. A group commitment to get out there and do something for a day that doesn't involve pursuing revenue (i.e., building a Habitat for Humanity residence) is good for the soul. Your people will feel a "business high" by giving back to the community, and so will you. Even if your company takes a more philanthropic approach by donating funds to help open a new hospital wing or department, it will still do your heart good to witness the final result when cutting that celebratory ribbon. Keeping your business heart brimming with community "oxygen" is part of a balanced lifestyle.

People do indeed enjoy making money, but it's not enough to distract them from the reality of too many deadlines, excessive hours, and not enough support. This leads to feeling "burnt out" from running for too long on the hamster exercise wheel. On the TV show *Mad Men*, the advertising industry of the 1960s is portrayed as a competitive, fast-moving, and sometimes-sleazy rat race. According to Wikipedia, a rat race "...is an endless, self-defeating, or pointless pursuit. It conjures up the image of the futile efforts of a lab rat trying to escape while running around a maze or wheel." I think it's fair to say this is the opposite of work-life balance, and not at all good for your heart.

What is the heart of your business? It should be your people, the culture you foster and perpetuate, the way you treat people both internal and external to your business. Are you fundamentally honest and ethical, or do you constantly screw people over in pursuit of even more monetary success? Are you capable of caring for others without demanding or expecting a "quid pro quo" (the Latin expression meaning "something for something") exchange in return? Do you treat some people better than others, or do you treat people as equally worthwhile human beings? And what is the voice of your customer?

Call it your social footprint if you like, but I view all this as part of your lifestyle balance, which includes giving back. Reasons for social mistrust of corporations and the relentless attack on capitalism (with all due respect to Ayn Rand and her portrayal of free market enterprise in *The Fountainhead* and *Atlas Shrugged*) include: decades of subliminal advertising, misrepresented information on product labels (especially food), and other questionable business practices. Whether your company is large or small, you have many targets to consider beyond your numbers. Goals regarding well-being, family, relationships, and community all matter to your company's heart health. The social responsibility aspect of your strategic plan should be as important as your financial ambitions. If you just talk about this key philosophical issue, but it doesn't drive your business, not all the chambers of your heart are pumping at full capacity.

We're now going to review your heart's basic structure. Unlike other human organs, the heart has multiple chambers. You have a right atrium, right ventricle, left atrium, and left ventricle. Like an uninterruptible power supply (UPS), both sets of chambers work to keep blood flowing through your body. The right atrium and ventricle work together to pump oxygen-depleted blood from your body to your lungs. The left atrium and ventricle work together to pump oxygenated blood from the lungs back into your body. I'm not a medical doctor, but I do know this: Without all four chambers of the human heart, you're dead. The same could be said regarding your business heart. Without what I consider the four chambers of a business's heart—people, culture, customers, and ethics—your business is "heart-dead."

Several immediate examples come to mind regarding corporations whose business hearts possess all four chambers. Companies that blend social responsibility into their business mantras include: Ben & Jerry's (the Ben & Jerry's Foundation), Tom's of Maine (50 States for Good™ and Dental Health for All™), Green Mountain Coffee Roasters (their Fair Trade and Sustainability programs), and the Campbell Soup Company (with their ten-year initiative to reduce childhood obesity in Camden, NJ). These companies and others continue to prove businesses of all sizes can be profitable and accountable at the same time. I honestly believe it's possible for your business to be even more profitable as a result of doing the right thing (thank you, Spike Lee) for both stakeholders and customers alike. So let's get into the "Zen" of maintaining a healthy, responsible heartbeat.

We've already discussed in previous chapters how to treat your employees well when using your business senses (vision, hearing, voice). By listening to and communicating with your people, your genuine concern for them strengthens your business heart. From an ethical viewpoint, you should always err on the side of doing right. Your mission statement and philosophy should be in line with your humanistic goals and communicated consistently throughout your company.

To keep the customer chamber of your heart healthy, it's important to know "likes and dislikes." Do you have Customer Relationship Management (CRM) software in place and update it regularly? If not, I recommend you do so. What charities do your customers or clients like and support? Are there opportunities for partnering your philanthropic interests with those of your customers and employees? At the end of the day, it is about running a business, but it's also about running a socially responsible business full of heart and soul.

And how well do you treat your suppliers? Are you willing to negotiate with them to maintain partnerships that foster mutual loyalty and empathy? This type of relationship should be built on "give and take," not mired in stubborn refusal or inflexibility, especially when the discussion involves reciprocity. I know I don't have to ask if you've ever heard of *The Godfather* movies. (Do I?) In the opening scene of *The Godfather*, Don Vito Corleone tells Bonasera (the undertaker) he can count on Vito's organization to take care of the thugs who beat up Bonasera's daughter. And in return: "Someday, and that day may never come, I'll call upon you to do a service for me. But until that day, accept this justice as a gift on my daughter's wedding day." Take a page from the notebook of the only Mafioso in this movie who dies of natural causes—know how to return a favor.

There was a time when business relationships were forged and agreed to on a handshake. When you don't pay your outside suppliers on time, it weakens them and poisons your business psyche. And really, what is the benefit, what do you actually get when you're as tough as Ebenezer Scrooge on a customer or supplier? If you do right by your suppliers and customers, these loyal foot soldiers will treat you well in the lean times. And trust me, there will be lean times.

So never burn a bridge behind you (and stay away from incendiary devices like matches and fireworks). Your business world is smaller than you know—don't ever think your reputation isn't established! Play nice in the sandbox, boys and girls. If necessary, read or revisit Robert Fulghum's tiny gem of a book, *All I Really Need to Know I Learned in Kindergarten*. I especially like this piece of wisdom: "Live a balanced life—learn some and drink some and draw some and paint some and sing and dance and play and work every day some." It's all about being respectful, kind, and understanding of others. That, and using your business voice…

Instead of bottling up your thoughts and feelings, which builds stress and can cause a physical heart attack, communicate. It seems to me it's always the quiet people who end up in the cardiac ICU. The stress that results from lack of communication can kill you, and it can also kill your business. People are at the heart of your business no matter what you produce and sell. By communicating well and building healthy relationships, you create an aura for your company that spreads and becomes the filter for how people perceive you. Business-planning expert Tim Berry explained the heart of a business (in 2007) as three concepts you should never pull apart: the market (knowing and understanding your customers), your identity (how you are different from others, your core competence, etc.), and focus (you can't do it all, so focus on your key target market). This conceptual trio should pump your business heart. But if your heart's chambers aren't pumping oxygenated blood, you have no circulatory health. In fact, the philosophical nature of your business's cardiovascular system complements and enhances the operational/transactional nature of circulation. By optimizing your business heart with a socially responsible fitness program, your employees will add all the new blood it needs to keep pumping.

My philosophy regarding business fitness is to perform at 100% of your maximum capacity. To maintain a healthy business heart, you need happy, engaged people working for you who enjoy a balanced lifestyle. What does this mean to you, my business-owner friend? It means you offer your employees a decent health care package that includes incentives such as a smoking-cessation program and flextime for exercise. One simple group activity to encourage is going for a walk at lunchtime during the week. Business is a contact sport, so you must come ready to play. You also must train to play well. I'll spare you the obligatory football analogy here.

The motivation for others in your company to achieve personal fitness starts with you. You need to lead by example, or all your talk about caring for the well-being of your employees isn't going to clear the first hurdle on your running track. If you belong to a gym or have an on-site fitness room, are you there in the morning? Do your people see you trickling with sweat as they struggle to incorporate more exercise into their lives? Do you give your fitness warriors a little extra time to work out during the lunch hour? People feel better and adapt a more positive attitude at work when they know you sincerely care about their health.

Additionally, being mentally "crisp" is another aspect of taking good care of your business heart. There are many tactics for encouraging clear, attentive thinking within your company: have water readily available; furnish the office with bowls of fresh fruit instead of obscenely large candy jars; for those midday meetings, bring in healthy lunches that don't come from Kentucky and aren't fried. Start an in-house newsletter (or outsource one) offering nutrition tips your people can easily implement at home. This heart-healthy strategy will transform your staff into a lean, mean, fighting machine of energy. The little things can make a big difference in creating a healthy work environment.

Have you ever heard of Feng Shui? C'mon now, it's the 21st century, so I know you have. This (3,000-year-old) ancient practice encourages balancing the energy contained by a space/room/place with the goal of enhancing health and good fortune for the people living or working there. Before you dismiss the concept of a yin-yang balance between water (the Feng part) and wind (the Shui part), take a painstaking look at your current physical work environment.

Do visitors see green plants, windows, natural light, and contemporary furniture when glancing into your world? Or is the view of your inner sanctum an outdated (and uncomfortable) "harvest gold and avocado" décor wheezing from old age? And if this environmental throwback to the 1970s or 1980s permeates your workplace, what does it communicate about your company's culture and your personal values? You don't have to be young to be socially hip!

When you invest in a healthy, comfortable work environment, it changes the whole company's ambience—it brings your entire workforce UP. You'll begin to notice fewer people sneaking out for cigarette breaks. The healthier lifestyle you introduce into your company's social structure will coerce your people to change for the better. The ones who can't abide such change will pack up their stuff and take their unhealthy ways with them as they leave. But I'm just warming up. There's more to a healthy business heart than what happens between the hours of nine and five.

I'm a true believer in the power of offering employees flextime. When you give the business gift of flexible hours, you're investing in the physical and mental health of your people. By being flexible, you communicate a welcome message—productivity doesn't necessarily happen between 9 a.m. and 5 p.m. The reality is that your employees hit their individual peak work performance at various times during a 24-hour cycle. Offering a flexible work schedule shows you trust your people to get the work done while enhancing their personal quality of life. This isn't stealing. This is you ensuring your business achieves optimal heart health.

You do want your employees to love coming to the office each day and enjoy working with you, don't you? Happy people who carry around less stress tend to perceive their employment as a great opportunity. Part of your job as a business owner is to reduce/remove the stress factors that contribute to heart disease. And while we're on the topic of removing stress, you are also the one responsible for eliminating political warfare from your work environment. Individual battles between certain employees are doomed to infiltrate your entire office and spread discontent. You need to shut down these psychological stressors—they can cause as much damage as physical stress. It's a known fact that too much stress of any type weakens the human heart, so it's good business to foster lifestyle balance at work daily.

When it comes to child-care issues, regardless of your personal beliefs regarding parenting, be flexible and take a step back. Your employees all have lives outside of work, but working parents in particular (or adult children giving care to elderly or disabled parents) need as much flexibility as you're willing to offer. The concept of "the human condition" goes something like this: We as human beings face endless situations in our struggle to get along with each other. You should pay attention to the human condition that exists within your company and cultivate a three-dimensional workplace. On a warm summer's day when the phones aren't ringing and the "smart" tablets aren't pinging, let your people play hooky and indulge in some fresh air (and an ice-cream cone). If you can, join them for this little escapade. And about those weekends: Expecting e-mail replies from your employees on a Saturday or Sunday just isn't fair. After all, it's YOUR business, not theirs. People instinctively want to like working for you, but that doesn't mean they desire your frenetic lifestyle as a business owner.

The accounting industry comes to mind when I think about a vivid example of employer flexibility. Accounting firms generally slacken the reins on their people from April 16th until the end of the calendar year. But during the sacrosanct time between January 1st and April 15th, accounting firms harness their CPAs and support staff like cattle in a holding pen. I guess what I'm saying is this: You shouldn't assume people will "slack off" without your watchful eyes on them, and you must reward them for their hard work.

It's true you provide the economic sustenance that allows employees to survive and remain above water. But your flexibility will build a stronger business heart and demonstrate respect for the work-life balance. Once you see how easy it is to make people happy, a healthy spirit of compromise will spread throughout your work environment. Let them come to work late, leave work a little early, or do what they've got to do in the middle of the day. The healthier your business heart is, the better your circulatory system will function.

We won't get into the bloody details (go ahead, laugh) of your company's circulatory system (i.e., transactional flow) until the next chapter. I'm mentioning it again because of this system's co-dependency with your business heart. Your heart is a strong muscle that functions as a nonstop pump. Your heartbeat is what stimulates the circulatory system of your business. Without a healthy heart, blood (which equates to cash flow) doesn't circulate throughout your business's body. No circulation means your company is about to experience cardiac arrest, which is more accurately referred to as cardiopulmonary arrest. According to most medical websites (and Wikipedia), cardiac arrest is "the cessation of normal circulation of the blood, due to failure of the heart to contract effectively." Remember my interpretation of your business heart's four chambers? Without ethics and a social connection to the world outside your business, you'll lose both employees and customers. Your business and its culture will perish. And once your business heart goes into cardiac arrest and stops, so will your cash flow. Before your heart starts palpitating too quickly, take a deep breath and relax. We'll get into the details of a healthy circulatory system soon enough.

I realize asking you to think like a "social entrepreneur" (rather than an old-school business entrepreneur) is a significant paradigm shift. Most business owners and CEOs are inclined to fill opportunity gaps in the marketplace with products or services that create profit. I'm suggesting you seek out those same openings in your industry and fill them with products or services that can also make a difference in people's lives. If you can't be the one to champion a socially responsible heartbeat, ask someone else in your organization to take charge of developing this shared-value mentality. If you own a large business, appoint someone from your

HR department. If your business is a smaller, "Mom and Pop" enterprise, perhaps the ally you seek is your office manager.

The rise of the "do-good," for-profit organization is a trend that's here to stay. There's no reason not to be a more socially responsible business owner. As always, I recommend you intermittently monitor your heart health by talking with your people about all the relationships supporting your business. Think of this as a stress test for detecting an abnormal rhythm or poor blood-flow to your business heart. Ask how well you're treating your community, the environment, and the world. As your company profits and succeeds, don't forget to "pay it forward" with a multitude of random acts of kindness. (Allegedly, writer Anne Herbert scribbled the following on a placemat back in the early 1980s while eating at a restaurant in Sausalito, CA: "Practice random kindness and senseless acts of beauty.")

Whether you want to call such acts good deeds or mitzvoth (the plural of mitzvah, a commandment), pump up your business heart's health by doing SOMETHING that isn't about pure profit. Perhaps your business is as successful as you think it is, but here's the question you want to ask yourself, Mr. or Ms. CEO: What is the legacy you want to leave behind associated with your name? Start pondering this question each day when you wake up. Now it's time for a heart-healthy story…

Chapter Six Story:

I already mentioned a few corporations that wear their business hearts on their sleeves, but one company with amazing heart and "soles" (as in the ones on your feet) is TOMS Shoes. Founded in 2006 by Blake Mycoskie (CEO and Chief Shoe Giver) and located in Santa Monica, CA, TOMS Shoes is the result of a fateful vacation in Argentina. While there, Blake Mycoskie noticed many Argentine polo players wearing canvas slip-on shoes called alpargatas, and he couldn't resist wearing a pair during his stay. While traveling around the country, Mr. Mycoskie noticed many children, most of them poor, facing multiple hardships on the streets of Buenos Aires.

One such observation was their lack of footwear—most of the children were shoeless. This may sound like an ideal situation when you're on vacation at a world-class beach resort. But being shoeless in a country like Argentina equates to possible exposure to soil-borne diseases and not attending school. Blake Mycoskie discovered lack of footwear was a significant childhood disadvantage all across Argentina and in other parts of the world. And so, he sourced and reached out to multiple Argentine shoe manufacturers. His goal was the creation of a for-profit shoe business (alpargata style) that would also put shoes on the feet of impoverished children in developing countries. Once the vacation was over, Mr. Mycoskie saw a brighter tomorrow on the horizon…

Okay, that was a somewhat odd transition, but I did it because the company's name comes from the word "tomorrow." Blake Mycoskie's original business concept was known as the "Shoes for Tomorrow Project." The philosophy by which he runs TOMS Shoes is "one for one." For every pair of shoes the company sells, it donates a free pair of shoes to a child in a developing country (Argentina, Haiti, Guatemala, and so on). TOMS sold 10,000 shoes in its first six months of operation, and that's exactly how many pairs of free shoes were handed out to Argentine children in October 2006.

Since that year, TOMS has distributed over two million new pairs of free shoes to children in need all over the world. But the company doesn't do this alone. TOMS makes a profit and gives back to the world with help from its customers, suppliers, and what the company calls its "Giving Partners." Their website proclaims, "With every product you purchase, TOMS will help a person in need. One for One®." Now that TOMS also manufactures and sells eyewear (glasses), a portion of each sales transaction is donated toward saving and restoring the eyesight of poor people in developing countries. TOMS Shoes has a business heartbeat made healthy by all four chambers pumping together: people, culture, customers, and ethics. So consider slipping on a pair of comfortable shoes and doing more business with companies that do good things for others. I'll leave you with a well-loved Winston Churchill quote: "We make a living by what we get, but we make a life by what we give."

Chapter Seven: The Circulatory System (transactional/electronic/human/financial flow)

As I mentioned in Chapter Six, the cardiovascular and circulatory systems are integral to each other, both in human and business bodies. They go together like love and marriage and, dare I say, like a horse and carriage. For those of you catching on to my corny reference, don't worry. I'm not about to insert the full song lyrics from that classic Frank Sinatra tune. For those who have no idea which song I'm referencing, go ahead and do a Google search on "most popular Frank Sinatra songs" right now if you're that curious. I'll be here when you return…

Circulation of blood in a human body should be free-flowing and continuous. Similarly, your business's circulatory system should be an efficient flow of transactional, electronic, human, sales/marketing, and financial processes. The healthier your business, the faster these internal processes will flow. The less healthy your business, the slower your processes will flow, due to what I'll call "gunky" blood. And if your business isn't healthy, trying to have all your internal processes flow quickly and efficiently is the equivalent of running through a pool filled with Jell-O®. Do you know now what I mean by "gunky?" I think you do. Let's wade through all the different processes that contribute to a business's good circulatory health.

If you're going to boost your business circulation, you need to emulate Maverick and Goose from the movie *Top Gun* by feeling "the need for speed." Organizations that process information and tasks efficiently (and in less time) can reduce their transactional costs. This is helpful when competing against others in your industry. Because technology has altered the speed of everything these days, each day is a race, and you know you need to be the swiftest. Questions should be answered more quickly. The number of layers between your employees and accomplishment of their tasks need to be minimized. The more people who touch a task or assignment, the more inefficiently and slowly your business's lifeblood circulates. Remember the telephone game ("Whisper down the Lane") I mentioned in Chapter One? Just as messages and communication can be distorted, the transfer of information by too many hands mucks things up. There's a price tag associated with multiple people touching the same report, presentation, proposal, or sales call. Your labor costs go up, and your ability to take new products or services to market slows down. This is not good. It's time for a circulatory check-up with Doctor Brad!

Your circulatory system isn't a standalone configuration. It actually consists of three unique systems that need each other and work together: the heart (cardiovascular), the lungs (pulmonary), and all the arteries, veins, and vessels (systemic) responsible for blood flow and distribution of nutrients and oxygen. Here's a statistic from Livescience.com that should impress you: "In the average human, about 2,000 gallons (7,572 liters) of blood travel daily through about 60,000 miles (96,560 kilometers) of blood vessels." This type of travel is much more efficient than taking a red-eye out of LAX (Los Angeles) on a Wednesday night.

Your heart is the center of your circulatory system. It is the motor. It is the pump that causes your circulatory system to endlessly push blood throughout your body. Circulation is a continuous process, not a start-and-stop type of action like eating or sleeping. The never-ending cycle of arteries carrying blood away from the heart, and veins carrying blood back to the heart, builds upon itself. This is why your business's circulatory system must be free of internal blockages. We'll discuss blockage issues in more detail momentarily.

Your human body's good or bad circulation is the product of your family history, what you put into your body for nutrition, and your activity/exercise regimen. The same is true of your business circulation. Accumulation of informational garbage, retention of people past their expiration dates, and obsolete technology slow down your business and damage your circulation. How quickly you service your customers regarding typical business requests is a tell-tale sign of good circulation. Let's say you're asked for a cost estimate. Do you bang it out and get the quote to your customer within 24 to 48 hours, or do you finally e-mail the quote several weeks later? Your transactional speed impacts how customers view you and your company, but accuracy is also important for good circulation. You don't want to stumble and fall down, especially if your business has hemophilia.

You probably know hemophiliacs suffer from a rare bleeding disorder—their blood doesn't clot properly. According to the National Heart, Lung, and Blood Institute, "If you have hemophilia, you may bleed for a longer time than others after an injury. You also may bleed inside your body (internally), especially in your knees, ankles, and elbows. This bleeding can damage your organs and tissues and may be life threatening." (Interesting fact: Because Queen Victoria of England was a carrier for hemophilia, and it's a known fact that those royal families from the 1700s and 1800s intermarried, this rare medical condition became known as "The Royal Disease.") Your options regarding business hemophilia are: improve your business circulation or never fall down, unless you want your company to bleed to death. And by this I mean losing profits because your sales cycle takes too long and eats money (rather than good nutrition). Let's apply some pressure and get into a flowing discussion regarding ways to optimize your transactional speed.

Remember Speedy Gonzales? He wasn't the most politically correct cartoon character to spring from the delirious minds at Warner Brothers (aka Looney Tunes/Merrie Melodies), but he certainly was believable as "The Fastest Mouse in All Mexico." His trademark phrase "¡Ándale! ¡Ándale! ¡Arriba!" roughly translates into "Go on! Go on! Up!" This is the mind-set you need for effective transactional speed in today's go-go-go world driven by online communication and social media. A customer's experience with you and the resulting word of mouth that circulates (get used to me using circulatory references in this chapter) across the social media cosmos carry more weight than you give them credit for. Now is not the time to emulate Speedy's cousin, Slowpoke Rodriguez (also known as "The Slowest Mouse in All Mexico.") If you want to maintain a healthy circulatory system, grab your sombrero and ándale!

Back in the (business) day, returning a client or prospective customer's phone call within 24 to 48 hours was considered reasonable. Not anymore. You know how you send your son or daughter a text message and get no response, but when one of them sends a text asking you for money, you're badgered for a response? That's because your children want immediate gratification (and money - ping! ping! ping!). Well, this communication model has transferred over to your work life. So the quicker you fulfill a request or reply to an inquiry and make it a good experience for customers and potential customers, the better your circulation will flow. Let's take a look at your online opt-in strategy.

Whether it's on your website, your landing page, your blog or elsewhere, your opt-in request (i.e., for building an online marketing list/database) needs to be minimal, not invasive. An opt-in asking for one or two pieces of information—typically, a name and e-mail address—is a much better plan than an opt-in asking for almost everything except someone's social security number. You need to layer how you request information for lead generation purposes from the seething, online masses. People just don't have the patience or time to input their demographic minutia, so be strategic. If prospective customers feel you're blocking their path, they will flick you out of the way. Where I come from, this attitude is considered a "New York mentality." New Yorkers (from the five boroughs) don't tolerate anyone or anything wasting their precious time. New Yorkers can seem rude to the unaware, but it's definitely much more of a "tough" or "survival mode" type of persona. Online, virtually everyone is an honorary New Yorker, so design your digital opt-in request thoughtfully.

Pick up your head and take notice of how business transactions move much more quickly online. The Internet has empowered anyone with a connection and a desktop, laptop, or mobile device to be able to access information in real time. "Click to chat" is another online feature capable of adding oomph to your transactions and revving up tired or slow circulation (Geritol®

joke deliberately omitted). If you're not familiar with this tool, it is software you embed into your website to provide customers and visitors with live, immediate assistance and information (by keyboard). You can offer "click to chat" on your company website from suppliers like LiveChat or BoldChat as an alternative to phone or e-mail. The unavoidable fact is this: To improve transactional speed and flow, you must get comfortable using and implementing current online solutions.

Proclaiming you don't understand all these fast-moving processes and options won't cut it anymore. If you don't follow the lead of online risk takers, you will get crushed. There's an expression of unknown origin (but probably a gift from the Deep South) that says "If you can't run with the big dogs, you'd better stay on the front porch." I'm sure there are variations to this piece of southern-fried advice, but the translation is universal—if you can't keep up with your competitors, don't bother trying. Instead, I'm sure you can make a tidy profit looking for buried treasure (and empty soda cans to recycle) with a metal detector on a crowded beach somewhere in Florida. Okay, that was sarcasm. It's time to OUTRUN the big dogs so they aren't adopted and fed by your best, most loyal customers.

No doubt about it: Technology has shifted the paradigm of client and customer expectations. The worst thing you can do is be inconsistent in your transactional process. I equate this to running a business like a money-back guarantee trap. During the heyday of direct response TV ads in the 1970s and 1980s (now known as infomercials), the "no-risk, 100% money-back guarantee" was one of the sneakiest ways to take consumers for a bumpy transactional ride. Companies were happy to receive people's $14.99 payments. But when disgruntled buyers tried returning (for example) a defective Thigh Master (no offense, Suzanne Somers), they didn't realize that the shipping and handling, sales tax, and other assorted fees weren't included in the refund. Beware being quick to take customers' money but slow to give it back if a full refund is warranted. I consider this a transactional blockage. Such blockage can only lead to one thing: circulatory illness.

You need to be fast and responsive at both ends of a transaction, unlike Comcast's turtle family of dial-up throwbacks, the Slowskys. Bill and Karolyn Slowsky have been taunting TV viewers with their preference for a super-slow, dial-up connection (rather than Comcast's super-fast broadband connection) since 2006. In fall 2013, the Slowskys became business owners with the opening of their restaurant, Slowsky's. When their nephew Kevin pleads for an upgrade to Comcast Business Internet, Bill and Karolyn suggest he take a break from trying to improve their operational efficiency. If you have transactional blockage because your business circulation is running on dial-up speed, expect your customers to crawl away from you way faster than the Slowskys.

Finally, your software configuration can either be an efficient example of circulatory health or an unwieldy process setting you up for transactional blockage. As a technology guy, a dirty little secret I know is that more than a few of my clients have transactional processes running separately from their computer system's software. They do this to get what they want, but it slows down the company's circulation. If it takes you three full days to process a customer order instead of less than 24 hours, your transactional speed is in danger of an arterial blockage. I suggest you evaluate your software. Identify ways to merge external workarounds into your computer system so business transactions flow better from start to finish. And if you're not already doing so, provide electronic purchase confirmations and status updates to your customers. These little touches will reassure them and are good indicators of a healthy circulation. Bottom line, keep your transactional speed moving!

So business transactions need to flow well, but what about your company's electronic speed? I'm talking about how timely and effectively you handle your e-mail replies as well as responses to Internet queries (e.g., from a contact submission form). It's good business to make it painless for longtime and potential customers to contact and/or connect with you through technology. Not responding to all those opted-in people who then ask questions about your company (or their most recent purchase) is bad business. This will damage your circulation full-stop. I mentioned this before in Chapter Five (The Vocal Cords/The Resonator System). Hiding behind your e-mails and dawdling for lack of a reasonable reply is no way to manage your business.

Miss Manners (aka Judith Martin, and she's still alive) and Emily Post (an entire entourage of Posts, mostly women, carry the torch of correct behavior) continue to advise people how to handle themselves in a variety of social situations. Similarly, there is an etiquette to the timeliness of your digital communication with customers. I think Miss Manners said it best in an interview back in 1995: "You can deny all you want that there is etiquette, and a lot of people do in everyday life. But if you behave in a way that offends the people you're trying to deal with, they will stop dealing with you..." The longer you continue to neither acknowledge nor answer someone's electronic inquiry, the greater the risk your customer (or employee) will assume you're deliberately ignoring them.

Of course, you must delicately balance between a timely response and providing the appropriate reply. This is why law firms include a disclaimer in small font on their websites or blogs or landing pages stating that the information you're reading should not be misconstrued as actual legal advice. As a CEO or business owner, it's up to you to ensure policies and procedures are in place for communicating electronically. I continue to be dismayed when my clients announce Internet usage rules for clamping down on pornography searches or bombard their employees with guidelines concerning their e-mail signature, but they can't be bothered to standardize a response time frame. This is a procedural mistake. When electronic speed is too slow, your clients and customers become angry. When electronic speed is too fast, unmonitored or inappropriate communication can cause a disruption, and your arteries might explode. Don't let your business circulation stew in a pressure cooker—improve it by creating online communication rules and applying them to everybody at your company.

Regarding that e-mail signature: don't leave it at the personal whim of each employee. Let them know how much information to include, which social media account links are acceptable, which version of the company logo to embed, and so on. If someone is going away on vacation and intends to activate an "out-of-office" reply, you should have a protocol in place for what the bounce-back e-mail should say. It's just as important to create and implement policies regarding answering of office phones and how quickly to return customer and inquiry calls. You want to do your best to mirror your clients' response-rate expectations. Electronic speed standards aren't a nuisance or nitpicking—they're your best defense. It's up to you to prevent the people representing your business to the outside world from saying the wrong thing in an e-mail and launching an unfiltered message that implodes multiple inboxes.

Another piece of e-mail minutia that pushes my circulation into overdrive is the now-infamous "Reply All" land mine. If some or most of the people included in an e-mail chain don't need the additional information, be kind to your digital environment and refuse to circulate electronic pollution. Once you click the tempting (and potentially dangerous) "Reply All" button, you unwittingly feed others' ability to disrupt circulation flow with too many of those empty "LOL" and "Thanks a lot!" platitudes. If you can, use Obi-Wan's Jedi mind trick to convince yourself that the "Reply All" button isn't the option you're searching for.

Related to the electronic "out-of-office" auto reply, it's also mandatory to have an out-of-office hierarchy in place so your outside connections don't feel like they've been banished to the "Island of Misfit Clients and Suppliers." It shouldn't matter that Sharon in Business Development isn't in the office today to process a customer order, quote, or question. Your response time to all such requests should follow a defined work flow. When someone vital to your company's daily circulation is out, a delayed or MIA response gives one of your competitors permission to hijack the sale or sabotage a hard-earned relationship. Always have a contingency plan in place so your electronic speed can expedite a transaction on any given day. Just remember: When you say you'll get back to your connections right away (by phone, by e-mail, by secret handshake, I don't care) but you don't, people will gradually trust you less and look for another business to fill their "hungry heart." (I ask you: where else but in New Jersey can you take a little poke at a Bruce Springsteen song lyric?)

Most of these speed/circulation tips focus on your external response rate to customers and suppliers. I mean, please—it's a given you need to reply more quickly than your competitors when a new sale or client account isn't a sure thing. Your external response rate must rise to a level of efficiency that isn't too quick or too slow. But guess what? Your internal response rate to employees is also a part of your business circulation. I think of this as your "human speed," and it's also in need of proper, unrestricted flow.

When a subordinate sends you what they consider an attention-worthy e-mail but you don't reply or provide an answer, there's a good chance that individual will feel ignored by you. This person might imagine various scenarios as to why you haven't responded. Unless you want to become your own internal blockage (serious cases will necessitate a trip to my triage center), instead of avoiding electronic communication, accept the responsibility and own it. If you can't provide a solution right now, send a timely reply indicating you don't have the answer yet but that you'll get back to the person soon. Don't ever leave someone who works for you unacknowledged because you're unsure of how to respond. Lack of communication is the quickest way to destroy company morale and circulate the perception that you just don't care. Your primary responsibility is to keep internal communication flowing in tandem with those valuable business transactions. Whether we're talking about your company's transactional, electronic or human speed, you should always be conscientious about your response rate by checking your pulse.

A healthy circulatory system indicates that you're quick: you're taking the correct action steps, you're making the right decisions, and you're not wasting blood flow on multiple or duplicated steps. You have no internal blockage. And let me tell you, avoiding a circulatory blockage is crucial. When someone you love has a blocked artery, they end up on the wrong end of a vascular clamp wielded by a reputable surgeon about to perform coronary bypass surgery. While bypass surgery does restore blood flow to your heart by diverting it around another section of your blocked artery, it isn't a permanent fix. Did you know most coronary bypass procedures last an average of 8 to 15 years? Translated to the business world, this means you can't continue to treat your corporate body so shoddily. The "surgical" workaround or secondary route around your blockage won't last forever. Rather than torturing your circulatory system with rerouted transactional flow and temporary fixes, you must stop putting garbage into your business system and get into shape. This is your circulatory moment of truth!

Again, not to alarm you, but according to the Centers for Disease Control and Prevention, most deaths in the United States are cardiovascular related. This fact tops other causes of death such as cancer and stroke. That "in the red" profit and loss statement (P&L) at the end of a year or the loss of your two largest, best client accounts is a business heart attack. This is your warning—a heart attack means you have blockage. If your circulation stops due to heart attack, your business is flat-lined. It's going to take more than a defibrillator to bring you back to life. You shouldn't have to suffer a business heart attack before paying better attention to your business's circulatory health. My mission here is complete if I've scared you enough to get your heart racing and your blood flowing. Now let's talk about your sales and marketing circulation.

Perhaps you're currently working (or previously worked) with a consultant whom you brought in to teach your sales team how to generate leads. We've all seen PowerPoint slides of the classic sales funnel. The shape alone implies you have to wade through the stranger-filled public swimming pool again and again before finding end-of-the-funnel bliss with those people destined to be your best clients or customers. Lead generation does feed your sales and marketing circulation, but it requires planning, not "Hail Mary" tactics that keep you trapped at the top of the funnel. The commonly held business wisdom of the 80/20 rule goes something like this: 20% of your customers generate 80% of your sales. I believe this ratio is fairly accurate. So, you should think about how you can make your efforts to acquire new business from people who don't yet know you as cost effective as possible. I need to ask you a question, Mr. or Ms. CEO: Are you a hunter, or are you a farmer?

If you're a business hunter, you emerge from your corporate cave on a regular basis, personal-sized battering ram in hand. You look for new customers by beating them senselessly with your primitive message. You attempt to drag them into your existing customer base by force. Because these folks don't know you at all and no one has introduced you to them, they're likely to run before you even begin swinging your "weapon." Personally, I don't enjoy working with business hunters—they're too aggressive and malnourished. I'd rather work with business farmers.

You know you're a business farmer if you can answer "yes" to the following questions: Do you plant seeds? Do you motivate and incentivize your sales and marketing people? Do you have a lead generation calendar and set realistic goals for your marketing campaigns? I don't want you to be Genghis Khan; I'd rather persuade you to be Johnny Appleseed. And yes, he was a real person—Johnny Appleseed was his nickname. John Chapman (1774 – 1845) was an American trailblazer and ardent nursery man. Born in Massachusetts, he traveled by foot to various states (Pennsylvania, Ohio, Indiana, Illinois, West Virginia), spreading the gospel of apples and promoting the planting of apple trees.

This was a man who understood the importance of planting seeds for future growth and sustainability. If it will help you to retain this particular tip, do a search on Johnny Appleseed, print out whichever version of his historical image you like best, and tape it onto a wall in your office you stare at daily. Planting seeds, especially those golden referrals from your existing clients (who love you and would push you out of harm's way from an oncoming car), is much better than going on safari for big game. Promoting your business shouldn't be a blood sport. I can't possibly improve upon John Jantsch's (Duct Tape Marketing) definition: "Marketing is: getting someone who has a need to know, like, and trust you."

Just because a prospective customer says he or she doesn't want to hear from you right now doesn't mean there will never be any interest. Quite frankly, the only lead I consider a dead lead is someone who is physically no longer alive. Your job as head cheerleader at your company is to create a social footprint that spreads your message and allows you to build an audience of people who will eventually buy from you. One way to improve your sales and marketing circulation is to align your marketing cycle with your target audience's buying cycle. This means you need to build meaningful relationships and file away tidbits of information that clue you into buying behavior (so you'll eventually convert leads into customers).

However, this strategy doesn't give you permission to be opportunistic—you want to nurture your leads, not stalk them. Don't chase a lead like you're pursuing a romantic relationship unbalanced by unrequited love. Do you really want to be associated with Glenn Close's character in the movie *Fatal Attraction*? An average lead needs to be touched at least 5 – 6 – 7 times before your prospect is ready to buy, so be patient. Never resort to boiling some kid's pet bunny in a large pot of water to penetrate a potential customer's radar screen!

And speaking of romantic relationships, there's the thrill of courting a new love, and then there's the satisfaction of nurturing an existing love to a deeper, more satisfying (and more profitable) level. I'm going to assume you've seen or heard of the 1992 film *Glengarry Glen Ross*, adapted from David Mamet's 1984 award-winning play. (Interesting aside: The play's name is a combination of two fictional real estate developments: Glengarry Highlands and Glen Ross Farms. You're welcome, Trivial Pursuit players.) The plot revolves around a group of edgy, desperate real estate salesmen who curse at and browbeat each other as they attempt to unload undesirable parcels of land onto unsuspecting potential buyers.

A key moment in the movie version is when "top gun" Blake (aka Alec Baldwin) swoops in and dangles a carrot meant to motivate these hungry professionals. After verbally abusing the sales team (with foul dialogue that's the hallmark of a David Mamet script or screenplay), Blake tells them there's a contest for obtaining access to the fresh Glengarry leads. Only the top two sales people will get these leads. Everyone else will be fired. I sure hope you don't run your business like it's a David Mamet play!

I don't know about you, but I'd rather nurture warm leads from existing clients and work my methodical system for converting leads into sales over time. Why risk your financial stability for the promise of "better" leads that may or may not have you chasing people with no intent to buy? The best way to strengthen your sales and marketing circulation (and avoid needing a blood transfusion) is to deepen those relationships with the 20% of your customers who already buy from you and enjoy working with your company.

In line with Malcolm X's famous quote from a speech he made in 1965, you should keep your most valuable customer relationships strong and long "by any means necessary." E-mails, newsletters, social media posts, word of mouth, phone calls, birthday cards, and more—the better your outbound client communication, the better your sales and marketing circulation will flow. There was a time when my consulting practice wasn't as lucrative as it is today. When cash flow was low (yes, we'll get to that soon), my small circle of loyal clients kept me and my fledgling business alive.

Now that my consulting business flourishes, I use personal touches to let my clients know how much I value their loyalty. Scattered throughout any given year, I reach out to clients with thoughtful and appropriate gifts, a lunch or dinner out, a round of golf on a sunny day, and so on. In this way, my clients know I'm always around and accessible when they need me. As the ultimate sign of trust, give your personal cell phone number to your inner circle of customers. If used at all, it will probably be sparingly. It's good for your clients to know they have you as a figurative security blanket. You're not so very different from the famous *shmatte* Linus van Pelt clings to in many of the "Peanuts" comic strips (its first appearance was in 1954). Hopefully, no one named Lucy or Snoopy will try pulling you away from your customers.

We've gotten to the final aspect of business circulation that's challenging for me to address in a humorous way: your financial cash flow. Without this cold, hard version of your circulatory system, there is no business. If you owe more than you bring in, you can't invest in your company. You can't buy inventory or hire people. You need to have POSITIVE cash flow, which means your red blood cells should be reproducing all the time and your blood should be circulating unimpeded. When I started E3 Consulting Partners, I didn't invest in my sales strategy or a timely marketing campaign—I bought furniture. As I enjoyed the view from my ultra-modern desk, comfortably seated in my fancy Herman Miller Aeron chair, I didn't have enough cash left to invest in resources that mattered more to my revenue growth (like office technology). Positive cash flow is the lifeblood of your business's circulatory system. Without it, my theoretical People-Process-Technology triangle doesn't exist, and neither does your company. Lack of financial circulation is a rusty "we're closed" sign hanging in your window. Even worse, you may be leaking blood (i.e., money).

If your financial circulation isn't moving so well, perhaps you've accidentally cut open an artery or suffered an aortic aneurysm. This sounds scary, but it's an appropriate analogy. The aorta is your body's main artery, so when a section of it is overstretched and weak, it can burst. Expect some serious internal bleeding (or worse). Once you start bleeding, your business's circulation slows down, and you'll continue to lose more money trying to fix the leak. You need more than a tourniquet to stanch the bleeding. You have only a certain amount of time allotted to rectify negative cash flow. If you can't figure out how to minimize your expenses, get your accountant in stat (this is a Code Blue—your accountant is the ER doctor on call) to scrutinize your purchases. Learn to buy supplies in bulk. Buy locally. Determine if you really need all that you purchase. When significant money has been spent on sales and marketing campaigns but there's no resulting ROI, analyze the situation to determine what went wrong. A blood transfusion will only help temporarily. You need positive cash flow!

If positive cash flow isn't a normal occurrence for your business, you need a bit of Rod Tidwell's passion (à la *Jerry McGuire*) to start flowing in your veins and arteries: "Anyone else would have left you by now, but I'm sticking with you. And if I have to ride your ass like Zorro, you're gonna show me the money." This is a crude but accurate way of saying that it all comes down to operational efficiency. How good are your accounts receivable and accounts payable policies?

Let's start with the most basic "no-no" regarding cash flow and collections: Why are you selling to customers who owe you money? If this is you, stop it now. Rather than waiting for payment in full (net 30, 60, or even 90 days), implement progressive/incremental billing across your client accounts to accelerate and strengthen cash flow. Remember, your payables should not be greater than your receivables. And you'll collect more cash if you do it yourself. If you spent money on equipment, on training, on 1,000 jiggly hula girl bobbleheads with your logo on it, whatever: pay your bills. If your accounts payable terms are net 30, bide your time until net 27 or 28 to pop that payment in the mail, or send it electronically by net 30.

The longer it takes you to pay bills and the shorter it takes you to collect what's owed to you, the healthier your company's blood flow will be. Check your corporate credit card company's policy regarding early payments. Take advantage of any discounts that make sense for your financials. My final suggestion isn't for everyone. If a short-term boost to your cash flow is all you need, consider accounts receivable financing, also known as factoring. This isn't a loan—factoring doesn't add any debt to your ledger or P&L statement. Basically, you sell your invoices to a factoring agent/company in exchange for an upfront advance on the total due. Do this only if you're having difficulty collecting from a handful of clients. You want vigorous blood flow, not a rerouted and tortured circulatory system. Now it's time to lower your blood pressure with a nice story…

Chapter Seven Story:

The best example I can give you of an organization with outstanding circulation is my daughter's field hockey team at Eastern Regional High School in Voorhees, NJ. These girls have been national field hockey champions for four years now, and they've won at least ten consecutive New Jersey State Interscholastic Athletic Association (NJSIAA) titles. Sure, they have talent (what parent wouldn't proudly say so?), but that's not all they have going for them. It's the way their coach has trained them to play the game—it's all about SPEED. All these girls do is run! The team members who are the best runners play the most, each and every game.

Speed is the key to this field hockey team's success, from summer training camp to after-school practices to crucial games that result in victory. If the coach senses a weakness in the line-up, she identifies it quickly so the team's pace and speed on the field remain constant. When sitting on the bench during a match, each player, including my daughter, knows when she is going in—there's no guesswork or surprises, barring an injured player. Everything is laid out, and it isn't questioned. That's speed. It's the continuous, ever-flowing cycle of how girls' field hockey is played at Eastern Regional High School. This is how each season progresses. The following year, it starts all over again, a continuous flow of talent and speed, free of blockage.

These girls weren't always state champions, but with the carefully planned processes their coach has in place, they will continue to succeed. Think of your company as the business equivalent of my daughter's field hockey team. With practice and conditioning, you gain speed. If you don't have to worry about how your processes circulate and the pace at which they move, you can focus more on the game with your brain. Just like the human body needs continuous blood flow to stay alive, your business needs a continuous flow of transactions, communication, sales & marketing, and cash to keep moving in the right direction.

Chapter Eight: The Muscular System (Your Business Acumen & Core Strength)

I have yet to start a chapter with fitness humor, so here we go: "What fits your busy schedule better, exercising one hour a day or being dead 24 hours a day?" I wish I could take credit for this, but I found it on www.leanhybridmuscle.com. Just for giggles, go the website so you can see the cartoon accompanying the snarky comment (Copyright 2003 by Randy Glasbergen), and then return here to continue reading. (Welcome back!) As a business owner, you possess something that will definitely be dead 24 hours a day without a daily workout: your business acumen muscle. It may not be as physically noticeable as the muscles within your human body, but if you don't train your business acumen, it will deteriorate. And muscle atrophy is one step on the path to an unhealthy business body.

According to Wikipedia, the muscular system "…is an organ system consisting of skeletal, smooth, and cardiac muscles. It permits movement of the body, maintains posture, and circulates blood throughout the body…Together with the skeletal system it forms the musculoskeletal system, which is responsible for movement of the human body." Your business acumen muscle is a strength that separates you from your competitors. I'm sure you've heard of the expression "No pain, no gain," but honestly, a CEO or business owner shouldn't be up all night worrying about customers' pain points.

What you should be focused on is the larger goal of moving your clients to the next level of success. To do this well, you must support a client like no one else can (or will). Your business acumen muscle should be primed. You also need strong financial muscles (i.e., your circulatory system and heartbeat working together) for healthy cash flow. Then you can create the motion necessary for sending the right signals to all your other business systems (your people, sales and marketing, transactional flow, customer and supplier relationships, etc.). In the immortal words of Austrian bodybuilders Hans and Franz (from that late-1980s *Saturday Night Live* skit), "[I] want to PUMP you up!" (So don't be a girly-man OR girly-woman…)

Your human muscles function in three overlapping ways: through physiological (muscle size), neurological (how strong or weak the signal is from the Central Nervous System [CNS] for muscle contraction), and mechanical strength (the muscle's angle of force, joint flexibility, etc.). Within your company, these various aspects of strength combine to display the flexing of your business acumen muscle. But your business muscles don't stay strong without some nutritional help. All the muscle cells in your body produce adenosine triphosphate (ATP)—chemical energy used to power movement (a bicep curl, a leg extension, etc.). Using your muscles burns up most of what you eat, which is why you've got to feed your business well. Everything your business takes in—people, information, and technology—should cause movement. Think of this movement as a business workout.

But if your business muscles aren't getting enough oxygen, you're probably on the verge of lactic acid buildup. During a weight-training workout, you might notice a burning sensation in your muscles (yet it isn't soreness). This means you need to take a break and rest up before your muscles shut down from too much effort too quickly. But it doesn't mean you stop exercising. Because the stronger your muscles, the better your cardiovascular health will be. And while your heart muscle contracts on its own (involuntarily), all your other muscles are controlled by your brain/CNS and are in need of some Tiger Woods "attitude."

I mention this both admired and humbled golf professional because his personal approach to growing his own muscular system is a good philosophy (even if I don't agree with how he's managed his personal life since 2009). Tiger believes in what's known as a "growth mind-set" (as opposed to a "fixed mind-set"), and you should too if you want your business muscles in top condition. At the start of his career, Tiger Woods didn't fixate on being a perfect specimen of an athlete with God-given talent. To this day, he still puts emphasis on learning new skills so he can challenge himself and improve his game. Consider adopting Tiger's philosophy as your own and train your business muscles for continuous improvement. Just don't commit adultery behind your lovely (Swedish former-model) spouse's back and store suggestive text messages that you shouldn't have sent in the first place.

I want you to build a stronger, better business foundation through practice and conditioning, but I also want you to be innovative about it. Soreness the next day after a weight-training session means you challenged your muscles. And that's okay—you deserve to rest in between workouts. (Instead of "No pain, no gain," let's change it to "No soreness, no gain.") But: If you use the same antiquated technology to process information since you started your business, if you resolve customer service issues using a three-ringed "policy binder" from 1979 as your guide, if you sit in a creaky swivel chair waiting for new accounts and clients to seek you out, you've plateaued. Not only are you not getting any new or improved results—your business muscles have atrophied. You're not using it, so you are definitely losing it!

The wasting away of muscle tissue because you're not stretching your business acumen is unacceptable. You need to challenge yourself, take action, and become more competitive. It's time to try something new and change your workout (or at least start exercising those puny muscles). If you can't be the one to investigate what it will take to increase your business muscle mass, hire someone to find out for you. That's right: I'm pulling you off the couch and drafting you into an emergency "boot camp" for wayward, diminished business bodies. (Go grab your water bottle and towel.)

The first thing you'll do during Coach Brad's Business Boot Camp is accept the weaknesses you have in your business. Once you do this, there's no need to revisit the other "stages of grief" that dragged you into your unhealthy state (i.e., denial, anger, bargaining, and depression). The next thing you'll do is find out the things you don't know so you can strengthen your business core and get moving. Because the truth is, you don't know everything—nobody does!

An initial way of stretching your business muscles is to obtain some education. Delve into new product research and development, read up on marketing trends and hot issues buzzing about in your industry, fill in your personal training gaps, and so on. For those of you who view business-networking gatherings as wasted time, get over yourself and RSVP selectively for networking events that provide opportunities to interact with other business owners. By networking with business-owner peers across different industries, you'll quickly discover how others are "exercising their muscles." To rebuild atrophied muscle mass, sign up for classes and workshops offering the appropriate "fuel" that can then be processed into business ATP. (Get moving—this is not a break.)

To strengthen your business muscles to maximum capacity, you must invest in your people. And not just any people: You need spindles of employee muscle that will challenge you to grow and expand your horizons as a leader. I realize you're now itching to know what a muscle spindle is. It's a sensory receptor that resides deep within the middle of a muscle. Spindles detect any change in a muscle's length and are important to muscle contraction and tone. They also contribute to proper functioning of your fine motor skills (such as hand and finger dexterity). In business terms, spindles are your people, so take good care of your business by diversifying your staff. Don't hire employees who are just like you and won't challenge your longtime business beliefs and practices. Recruit and hire new employees who have expertise in areas where you don't. When you bring in fresh talent complementing your areas of expertise, you strengthen your core muscles. (Good job! Take a long sip from your water bottle and get ready for some core training.)

When it comes to strength conditioning, a business owner or CEO must never get comfortable and settle into the same daily routine. When you reach a goal, don't proceed to park yourself on the couch, crack open a can of fizzy high-fructose corn syrup, rip open a bag of salty, processed carbohydrates and get flabby. The best way to strengthen your core muscles is by being (or becoming) ACTIVE. Grow your business muscles with good nutrition that feeds your company's People-Process-Technology triangle. As we discussed in Chapter Two, your digestive system needs to absorb useful, actionable information and eliminate what it doesn't need.

Your business body's systems must function at optimal health to create the energy necessary for flexing and then resting your muscles. But you know what? Having business systems in place doesn't guarantee good health. No one wants to "date" an overweight, sloppy business owner. Sure, you want to be attractive to potential customers, but it's your foundation that keeps your business strong and stable, not your pretty face. Let's discuss the difference between vanity and core muscles.

Many people I see "grinding it out" at the gym tend to focus on what I like to call their vanity muscles. The usual suspects include: your pectorals (chest), biceps, triceps, deltoids (shoulders), and your (hallucinatory) abdominal six-pack. These are the upper-body muscles that reside above your hips and waist. No offense, gentlemen, but many of you are notorious for ignoring your stabilizing core muscles (your abdominals and obliques, back muscles, and leg muscles) and overtraining your upper body. All I have to see are your matchstick-looking legs underneath an outdated (leather) weight belt to know your foundation is as weak as chamomile tea. Ladies, a lot of you do hundreds of crunches for your abdominals and focus on lifting the buttocks, but you may not necessarily be strengthening your stabilizing leg (quadriceps, hamstrings) and back (trapezius, rhomboids) muscles. Bundle all your business strengths together by including your stabilizing muscles when you train. This is your business's core. This is your foundation. And your business's foundation contains an important muscle that separates you from your competition, making your company stand out: your core differentiator.

You see, businesses across many industries each have a different muscle as their core differentiator. A quick example: Apple is typically thought of as a company with extremely strong leadership muscle. The company's overall muscle tone is balanced and natural looking, but when I say "Apple," the business world says "thought leader." You need to determine what your core differentiator is. Is it your sales process? Is it your well-fed and pumped marketing strategy? Is it the way each person working for you seeks out opportunities to burnish your company's reputation? A healthy business continues to train all of its muscles for balance and stability, but the muscle it should flex and strengthen most often is its core differentiator. (Lift that dumbbell in front of you—we're going to pump this one up a bit more.)

Your company's core differentiator is your story. It's who you are, what you live every day and sleep every night. It's why your clients need you. While you need overall muscle tone for good health and an active life, your core differentiator is your particular vanity muscle. No one can dispute it or break it down, but you must flex it before your competitors flex theirs. Companies with a strong differentiator are in the enviable position of teaching others how to "do it" well. As Carly Simon sang so soulfully in the theme song ("Nobody Does It Better") for *The Spy Who Loved Me* (what a classic James Bond flick from 1977!), "…nobody does it quite the way you do, why'd you have to be so good?" By distinguishing your business, customers will really have no other choice in your product/service category. The Walt Disney Company is equated with family entertainment. It pains me to say this, but for cheap, tasty hamburgers, McDonald's rules supreme. I ask if you want to grab a cup of coffee with me, and you tap "Starbucks within five miles of…" into your smartphone. Identify your business's strongest asset and exercise it every day.

Here's a theoretical example: You're lucky enough to land an appointment (i.e., sales call) with a desirable prospective client's top decision maker. The first question asked is, "How can you help me?" If at this point you launch into a canned/pre-packaged sales spiel that douses your target with a stream of generalities, you are not using your core differentiator. What I expect will happen next is this: Mr. or Ms. Decision Maker will cleverly signal to his or her administrative assistant, who will then say an important call is coming in during your pitch. And that's the ballgame, because you didn't get past the 15-minute hurdle. You need to go back to the gym and rack up more training hours to strengthen your core differentiator. Get rid of the flab on your business body.

Here's how the meeting should go: In response to that first important question, you provide insight regarding how you would resolve the prospect's problem, which you researched before the meeting. Your new best friend forever (BFF) looks you in the eye and says, "Tell me more." Ten minutes become thirty minutes. Before you know it, you've got a follow-up meeting scheduled for next week. And you'll be bringing with you the account/project manager who will service this new customer. When you lead with your core differentiator, you look and feel like a winner. You're offering your product or service in a way that allows prospective buyers to perceive just how much value you will add to their bottom line. You know before you walk into any prospective client's office exactly how you can help them. Once you are deemed valuable, you flex your business acumen further by sharpening your product/service offerings. (So don't head for the locker room just yet—this workout session isn't over.)

Sharpening your business offerings is similar to strengthening your core differentiator, but the process requires a few additional pieces of exercise equipment. Focus groups and/or survey research are reliable methods for tinkering with product depth and breadth. And by joining a business-building club (also known as a mastermind group), you'll gain brainstorming stimulation, education, and peer accountability. This isn't a class or group coaching—the other members will challenge you to set meaningful goals and then accomplish them. Also consider joining business societies and associations related to your core differentiator. Get active by volunteering to chair a panel discussion, business expo, or other event. Of course, listening is as important as doing.

I know we already discussed your auditory system back in Chapter Four, but listening is a skill that must be sharpened regularly like an expensive set of Wüsthof or Shun knives from Williams-Sonoma. Set up listening posts via your social media accounts and/or Google to track key trends, events, and innovations relevant to your industry. I know it's tough to keep up with the evolution of Google's "Everlasting Gobstopper" of an algorithm (Pandas and Penguins and Hummingbirds—oh my), but the next wave of influence on your business's digital life is all about authority. You want your website, blog, and/or social-media presence to rank higher in conjunction with the natural progression of search engine optimization (SEO). Position yourself so that others will seek you out and come to you as the go-to subject matter expert in your business community. Feed your "Google muscle" (you read it here first) meaty, satisfying marketing content that incorporates acknowledged sources and quality, non-spammy links. Look outside your business and listen to what's going on.

(No, that wasn't meant to be a Marvin Gaye reference, but "don't punish me [or your business muscles] with brutality.")

When sharpening your product/service menu, a nice balance between macroeconomic and microeconomic strategies is ideal. Macro issues that impact your niche should be listened to and absorbed: national economic circumstances, global supplier news, and world events that can affect your bottom line. On the micro level, pay attention to local government policies and business forecasts. Talk to the economic leaders who shape the demographics of your region. Take it all in and turn this "nutrition" into energy and ATP. Then change your strategic position by flexing your toned muscles (if that's what your brain is telling you to do).

Muscle conditioning by listening should be as compulsive as brushing your teeth. You need to do it at least twice a day (and don't forget to floss—your dentist will thank me), so allocate time for pumping up your products or services regularly. I want you to know EVERYTHING and have unlimited knowledge and awareness when it comes to what you sell or service for a living. I want you to be omniscient! (You don't have to look up this word—I just defined it for you.)

A great way to achieve universal knowledge and sharpen your offerings is by understanding your customers' needs and wants. I help my own clients become omniscient with an exercise I call "The Voice of the Customer." This involves reaching out to a cross section of your customer base (both satisfied and not so satisfied) and asking a series of very specific questions. (I prefer phone conversations, but select your communicative method based on customer preference.) Please commit these to memory or a file on your computer/tablet:

How did you find us?

Why did you buy from/hire us?

When during the decision-making cycle did you know you would buy from/hire us?

What can we do better?

What don't/didn't you like about doing business with us?

If you were to Google us, what words/phrases would you use to search for us online?

These questions work together to provide you with direct, valuable customer feedback that will strengthen your business acumen muscle and sharpen your product/service offerings. It's all about continuous improvement. Any decent personal trainer at a gym or other fitness facility will develop a regimen for you focused on gradual, incremental progress, not radical improvement within a few weeks. I believe the long-term goal of physical bodybuilding is to increase muscle tone and strength. Increased muscle size may be an initial goal, depending where your company is in its life cycle.

In the "muscle life cycle" of a business start-up, you must first build muscle mass (i.e., gain size) before you can tone and maintain your core differentiator. If you've been in business for five years or longer, you should already have a defining characteristic that distinguishes your business from its competitors, and it better not be your customer service. Because I've got news for you, my CEO/master commander/U-boat captain/leader-of-the-pack friend—excellent service is an expectation, not a core differentiator. If you can't figure out how to strengthen your business muscles, a personal trainer will coerce your business body to move and grow.

Your business "trainer" (i.e., business coach or consultant) will push you harder than you push yourself. A skilled trainer will also point out your weaknesses and put together a nutritional plan for strengthening your muscles. Someone not internal to your company offers a fresh, unbiased perspective regarding how you run your company. This person can observe what's going on (there I go again—thanks, Marvin). He or she will tell you things you may not know or realize about your own business that you should do differently or better. Your trainer will guide you toward improvement of the processes important to your company's sustained growth and success (e.g., our discussions regarding resolution of "useful versus useless" data/information flow [the Digestive System] and positive cash flow [the Circulatory System], etc.). And of course, a trainer will measure your progress over a defined period of time and change your routine when it looks like you're about to plateau.

On a personal note, I can't emphasize enough how critical it is to maintain good physical health through exercise and nutrition. Trainers and coaches will gladly provide the motivation if you can't spark it yourself, but you're the only one capable of making a deliberate decision to take care of your human body.

How you live and how often you incorporate fitness into your personal life spills over into your business life. Choosing a healthy lifestyle is a reflection on your business. Most people like to believe they lead an ethical, decent life. They don't cheat, steal or lie (unlike Scarlett O'Hara when she journeys home to Tara after the burning of Atlanta), and they pay their taxes on time. Choose to live a decent business life. Strengthen your professional muscles and tone your total business body by maintaining your core differentiator. Work out like an elite bodybuilder and think like a power player. If you live in the southern New Jersey area, walk into Ponzio's Diner (on Route 70 in Cherry Hill) at 6:30 a.m. on any weekday. Here's what you'll see: the cream of the local business community flexing their muscles by sealing lucrative deals while they fuel themselves for the day. Okay, you can take a break now—it's story time.

Chapter Eight Story:

I started working out (as in exercising) ten years ago, and it's the best business decision I ever made. My lifestyle choice is to exercise every day. It's an appointment I keep with myself to strengthen and take good care of my most important asset: ME. Without me, there isn't any business, and there isn't anything else. If you're not disciplined enough to do it yourself, find someone to help you, and invest your time in activities you'll actually enjoy.

Since that fateful day when I began to change my business by changing my body, no colds or viruses have yet to deter my progress. I used to get sick frequently and remain that way for a week at a time. Before incorporating fitness into my daily schedule, my outlook on life was mediocre. I'll admit it—my attitude was not the best. The energy and strength I gain from physical activity allows me to do two-to-three times more than most people can during one business day. The secret to my workout results is muscle confusion.

Whether I'm at the gym with my trainer or I'm going it alone, I never get comfortable with my exercise routine. I always vary my workouts. Sometimes I'll focus on a single body part, sometimes I don't use any weights at all, and sometimes I do full-body circuit training (this means I do one exercise per muscle group using a heavy weight load). The funny thing is, each time I finish challenging my muscles and churning up a little lactic acid, I'm not exactly sure what a particular workout will do for me, but I know I feel good. I'm not looking to achieve vanity muscles that would remind you of Arnold Schwarzenegger during his "Mr. Olympia" days in the 1970s. But Arnold knew what he was talking about in the 1977 movie *Pumping Iron* when he described "The Pump": "…Let's say you train your biceps. Blood is rushing into your muscles, and that's what we call The Pump. Your muscles get a really tight feeling, like your skin is going to explode any minute, and it's really tight—it's like somebody blowing air into it, into your muscle. It just blows up, and it feels really different. It feels fantastic." I don't know about you, but I like feeling fantastic.

Listen, I'm fairly confident you know how important physical fitness is for optimal health. I use muscle confusion and other related activities to maintain balanced muscle tone so I can live and work well. I don't want you to settle for the "97-pound weakling" type of existence Charles Atlas attacked so brilliantly in those cheesy ads he ran in comic books (starting way back in the 1940s) to sell his weight-training program. Just like Charles used to say, "Let ME PROVE I can make you a New Man [or Woman]!" Flex your business muscles and GET MOVING.

Chapter Nine: The Skeletal System (Your Structure and Infrastructure)

When you attended high school, you probably read John Steinbeck's classic novella about the human condition and loneliness, *Of Mice and Men*. But guess what? Mr. Steinbeck, as superb a writer as he was, lifted the book's title from a 1785 poem by Scottish poet Robert Burns. The poem is entitled "To a Mouse, on Turning Her Up in Her Nest with the Plough." Here's the famous stanza that inspired Steinbeck's liberal borrowing: "The best-laid schemes o' mice an' men / Gang aft agley, / An' lea'e us nought but grief an' pain, / For promis'd joy!" Why am I now Professor Tornberg of Business Fitness University? Well, sometimes your best-laid plans as a business owner or CEO (deals you make verbally, contracts you sign, etc.) cause you to trip over yourself incessantly. This tells me your operational fitness might be deficient. In the human body, this could lead to a broken leg or arm, compromising your ability to move and do things. In the business body, it's the equivalent of a weak structure (people and processes) and infrastructure (technology).

Without a strong business skeletal system protecting your "internal organs," your plans will often go astray, leaving you with nothing but grief and pain. The building in which your business physically resides is a structure, but it's only a shell when compared with your business operations and procedures. If your infrastructure doesn't enhance your work processes or support and promote the business activities of your people, your skeletal system has problems. One small example would be your Accounts Payable and Accounts Receivable staff having a custom computer configuration for their database(s). But when someone from this group needs to send data to another department, he or she manually downloads the information to a spreadsheet. This tells me there's a weakness in your skeletal structure.

Think of your business's skeletal system as a wire carrying electronic signals from your business muscles. Without a strong signal (i.e., your business processes), there is a disconnection between bones and muscles. You have no underlying structure in place. No structure all but ensures your employees don't communicate in a consistent manner. Lack of structure also negatively impacts the various business "speeds" we discussed in the Circulatory System (transactional speed, cash speed, etc.). A weak skeletal system leaves all your other business body's systems vulnerable to breaks, which can lead to inactivity. Think about it. Your muscles, bones, and joints work together. The human result is MOVEMENT.

All your primary "soft" organs are protected by some part of your skeleton: Your brain is protected by your skull; your spinal cord (Central Nervous System) is protected by your spinal column; your heart, lungs, liver and spleen are protected by your rib cage; your bladder and intestines are protected by your pelvic bones. Strong bones are a good indicator of a healthy body. Weak bones or the presence of bone disease indicate deterioration of the body. When was the last time you checked your business hips for proper alignment? Let's examine some of the cascading effects of an unhealthy skeletal structure.

When the bones in your human body are weak, you face all sorts of future health problems. Women of a certain age fear receiving a diagnosis of osteoporosis. This is a post-menopausal disease that diminishes bone density and leaves you more susceptible to fractures and breaks, especially if you fall. While osteoporosis is thought of as a women's disease, some men can also lose bone density in their later years and become vulnerable to breaks and fractures. Ladies, another skeletal issue you face later in life is kyphosis, also known as "Dowager's Hump" (i.e., hunchback). The severe rounding-over of your back means you have advanced osteoporosis. When you're young, you don't think about bone density because you assume your skeletal structure is as strong as it needs to be. But structural strength is all about proactive care, whether we're talking about a body or a business. You incorporate bone-friendly supplements (calcium, vitamin D to help with calcium absorption, vitamin K to direct where the calcium goes) into your diet and weight-bearing exercise into your lifestyle to prevent or reduce osteoporosis. Similarly, one of your executive responsibilities is to build (and sustain) a strong business structure. You must feed it good nutrition, ingest supplements and vitamins as needed, and challenge your structure with exercise to make it strong. Of course, sometimes you have to break a bone and reset it so it can heal properly.

I'm not referring to a troublesome fibula (calf bone) or a metatarsal (one of your foot bones). I'm actually talking about whichever cracked or fractured bone in your business structure is slowing you down. The most common problem I see at my orthopedic clinic is more detrimental than you realize: it's the "that's the way we've always done it" stress fracture (a repetitive injury). If this is your problem, you are managing your business while limping, my friend. Sure, your business acclimates and gets used to hobbling along with an unhealthy, weak frame, but it will never heal properly. Let's pretend your business is a skeletal cadaver and break it apart so we can more closely examine the assets that make it whole. We're about to take an X-ray of your business bones—your people, processes, and technology.

The business skeleton consists of two types of bones: a structure (people and processes) and an infrastructure (technology/IT systems). When you avoid improving business processes or empowering employees, you are setting your company up for a break or stress fracture. The information in your digestive tract should be shared and able to move up, down, and sideways when necessary. (Too bad Willy Wonka's glass elevator isn't real!) Don't overburden your people with heavy, endless business meetings. You want lean muscle making your processes agile, not informational fat clogging your arteries.

And don't forget: People impact your processes by how they embrace or reject the operational changes you are supposed to diligently manage. Change isn't easy, but it should flow up and down, not just from the top down like an avalanche sweeping all in its path to the bottom of a mountain. Information as well as employee suggestions should move in multiple directions for good bone strength. If you as a leader are too insecure to appreciate suggestions from your most junior employee and allow innovative ideas to flow upward, you're part of your company's structural weakness. You won't have the kind of people necessary for building a healthy business skeleton if you discourage employees from speaking up. Strong people and efficient processes make for resilient bones. But your skeletal system isn't complete without a well-cared-for infrastructure.

According to thefreedictionary.com, "the term 'infrastructure' has been used since 1927 to refer collectively to the roads, bridges, rail lines, and similar public works that are required for an industrial economy, or a portion of it, to function." Think of your business as the industrial economy and your IT systems as the roads, bridges, and rail lines. I defy you to maintain skeletal health without a reliable and compatible hardware/software configuration. I'll guess that some (if not most) of you are running an older computer system badly in need of updating and upgrading. Your company's mismatched hardware and software don't work well together because they're second or third cousins, twice removed. I'm not exaggerating when I say this is like taking a Lamborghini Aventador (amuse yourself for a moment at lamborghini.com) for a drive on a dirt road. Outdated desktops or laptops aren't meant to run the latest, greatest version of MS Excel or Access. Your infrastructure should be viewed as an investment in good skeletal health, not an unnecessary expense. Stop taking your structural fitness for granted like you did when you were a teenager or young adult. You might need more than a simple X-ray—I'm scheduling you for a DEXA Scan to determine your business's bone density.

A DEXA Scan (Dual Energy X-ray Absorptiometry) is a test to determine how much calcium (and other minerals) your bones contain. The resulting report identifies three levels of bone health: normal bone density, low bone density (referred to as osteopenia) and, the diagnosis you should dread hearing, osteoporosis. If we take a DEXA Scan of your business and the results show osteoporosis, I would advise you to start a supplemental program to invest more dollars into your infrastructure, processes, and staff. If you don't change your regimen soon, you will continue to weaken your skeletal system. You should be able to guess what comes next. Your business is going to fall, and something will break—perhaps your hip bone.

This is definitely not good. Here's a disheartening fact from the Centers for Disease Control and Prevention website: "Death rates from unintentional falls among older persons have increased since 1993." The good news is that osteoporosis can be reduced and curbed with good nutrition and exercise. Please step onto Doctor Brad's calibrated scale for a moment...

Is it possible your business is carrying too much weight? Does it have more fat than lean muscle? A bloated business can end up with knees too weak or unstable to support its weight. Avoid becoming a candidate for knee-replacement surgery. Strengthen those knees by supporting the people below you (in status/title) with "soft skills" that promote good bone density. Strengthen your conflict-resolution, decision-making, and listening abilities. Similar to the way people can be big-boned or have a small frame, businesses have differing skeletal sizes with unique issues or challenges to overcome. Small businesses and start-ups initially build muscle to be able to compete with larger companies for more profitable business deals. Big-boned companies may already have muscular strength, but without proper care of infrastructure, those larger, older frames aren't fully protected from business osteoporosis. The consequences of your business having a weak skeletal system could force your staff to hobble about on "workaround" crutches for a long time. Let's talk about what happens AFTER you fall and break something.

Once you do break a business bone—let's say it's your femur (thigh bone)—your business won't function at 100%, not with a broken leg. This injury prevents you from running or even walking correctly. Everything slows down, causing significant inactivity. Your loss of mobility (i.e., momentum) results in unhappy clients and employees. Inactivity creates an environment that is not a pleasant place to work in at all. A salesperson who can't collect his commission because your obsolete or cobbled-together computer system doesn't tabulate his monthly numbers accurately (and produce a check or direct deposit payment) won't tolerate this for long. In a company with a structurally weak People-Process-Technology triangle, the strong employees will leave—guaranteed. Your business's skeletal system protects your business "innards," but without strong bones working in unison with your business muscles, the other systems won't function well. Lack of movement impacts your HR heartbeat, your digestion of information, your circulatory speed (processes, transactions, financial), and so on.

Worst of all, brittle bones leave your business unable to compete in your niche or industry against companies with much better bone density. Damaged business legs destroy your agility. You can't make "quick cuts" the way a running back zigzags with the grace of a gazelle across a football field. All the winning qualities you possess won't help you stay in front of the competition if your sales and marketing warriors look and function more like a skeletal crew.

Have you ever seen the 1963 movie *Jason and the Argonauts*? At the very end of this interpretation of the Jason-and-Medea story (from Greek mythology) is a most amazing film sequence. It is signature work by the now-deceased master of stop-motion special effects, Ray Harryhausen. Basically, Jason and some of his men have stolen the much-coveted Golden Fleece and are trying to get back to their ship, but a small army (of seven skeletons armed with swords and shields) is in bone-rattling pursuit. The skeletons seem immune to all human effort to "kill" them. Jason is the last mortal standing so, in an effort to escape, he heads for the sea by jumping off a cliff. Ordered by vengeful King Aeetes to kill Jason, the skeletons follow him into the sea. But you know what's coming next—the skeletons lose their magic upon impact with the water (too much sodium for those crazy bones to handle). Their exposed bones couldn't fulfill the task. Don't let your business's structure or infrastructure decompose into a debris field of drifting bones, leaving your assets unprotected. It's never too late to improve poor bone density. Invest in your business's structural health!

The primary way to build a strong business infrastructure is by investing in the best technology for your people's needs. I will tell you again—stop viewing your IT infrastructure as an expense. Yes, you do have to pay for it, but technology (and all that it allows your employees to do faster and with more accuracy) is an investment. A healthy business supports its infrastructure in various ways. At the bare minimum, you should be backing up your computer systems weekly or daily (to a removable device that can be stored offline, or to a remote location) to guard against either an act of God or human error wiping out your hard drive. The flip side of system back-ups is having a disaster-recovery plan in place. After you identify the IT services critical to keeping your business circulation healthy (by doing a risk assessment), your disaster recovery plan should include strategies for prevention, response, and recovery.

Another element of structural integrity I mentioned earlier is change management. You are the one responsible for managing IT upgrades and process modifications. Remember, your business's infrastructure must carry and support the weight of your entire organization. You may have cardiovascular health, but you can't run with a bum knee. Build out your systems and processes, and build them better than whatever your competitors are using. Think of educational seminars, training, and continuous improvement as the supplements necessary to maintain a healthy infrastructure. And listen to your people when they tell you a process or IT device or piece of software isn't working as it should. Without such crucial feedback, you're an empty business brain in search of a body. Don't be a business zombie!

Speaking of bodies, your physical skeleton is one well-constructed, amazing piece of machinery. The smallest bones in your human body produce substantial motion and are responsible for just about all of your fine motor skills (all the small movements of your hands, wrists, fingers, feet, and toes). The theoretical "fingers" working tirelessly on your company's behalf are your people. And if your employees are the fingers of your business skeleton, you are the big toe (aka the hallux bone). Do you remember what Bill Murray's character said about his platoon leader, Sergeant Hulka, in the movie *Stripes*? Here's a comedic quip that applies quite well to the business world: "An army without leaders is like a foot without a big toe. And Sergeant Hulka isn't always gonna be here to be that big toe for us. I think that we owe a big round of applause to our newest, bestest buddy, and big toe ... Sergeant Hulka." Be the smartest big toe in your industry, and take good care of your smaller, hardest-working bones. Extremity injuries are the worst!

Sustaining an injury to a finger or toe will impair your business's performance and dexterity. When you fracture or break these smallest of business bones, all of a sudden, it's impossible to perform all the fine motor skills you take for granted: entering information into a database, picking up a pen to write, driving to an important meeting or presentation and, oh yeah, walking. The rest of your company will compensate for an injury and, eventually, the pain will subside, but bones won't heal better and return to full strength unless your business is already in good shape. If you still aren't incorporating weight-bearing exercise into your business routine, if you aren't training your business muscles, then your bones will never achieve optimal strength. There's a reason medical anatomy books refer to it as the musculoskeletal system. Muscles and bones are interrelated. And muscles, tendons, and ligaments work together with the bones to propel your business body FORWARD.

While the human skeletal system protects your internal organs, it is also the catalyst for muscle contraction. Each time you go for a walk or work out with weights or swim some laps, your muscles and bones pull together to make each movement happen. Muscles are attached to bones. Without your skeletal framework, you can't build muscle. Without a strong business structure (your people and processes bones) and infrastructure (your technology bones), you can't maintain strong business muscles. From an anatomical perspective, it's muscle that supports the human skeleton. From a business perspective, it's your structure and infrastructure supporting your ability to "be strong" for your customers and deliver what you promised them, whether it's an improved product, a more innovative service, or something else.

If the skeletal structure of your PPT triangle is strong, you can act quickly. You can execute decisions and change direction as necessary without compromising the integrity of such decisions. But don't neglect to exercise your musculoskeletal system, and don't forget to take supplements if you need them for better business bone density. When you willingly invest in your structure and infrastructure, you reduce the possibility of muscle tearing from bone, an incredibly painful injury with a long recovery time. Keep your business bones strong!

Before we get to the story, let me reiterate the consequences of a calcium-depleted operational skeleton so you'll heed my orthopedic advice. Operationally weak companies…

…don't make enough or any money.
…produce inferior, poor products.
…lose good, talented, strong people.
…waste time doing lots of manual data/information processing.

...have leaders who don't acknowledge their own blemishes and deficiencies.

Operationally weak businesses are literally trapped in a body cast: there's no movement. The owners of such businesses compel their people to resort to using workarounds for bad, dysfunctional processes and outdated IT systems. Accompanying this operational paralysis is the lack of formal change management procedures in place to encourage employees' acceptance and implementation of change. Your company will never move as fluidly as you desperately want it to until you stop having a knee-jerk reaction to the word "expense" and start investing in your company. Please stop repeatedly fracturing your clavicle. This has nothing to do with your neck—these are the two long collarbones just underneath your neck that connect your breastbone to the shoulder blades. A collarbone break is very common among athletes, and it usually heals on its own (in about 6-12 weeks). But if your business doesn't have a strong skeletal system, it will probably continue to break a collarbone. Repetitive injuries never heal properly...

Chapter Nine Story:

I have one particular client with a collarbone that will never mend. The source of the injury is a key member of management whose dysfunctional behavior reveals a level of insecurity and lack of organizational structure that are monumental. This company has plowed its way through four comptrollers in one year. (I'm getting queasy just telling you about it.) Why has this happened? It's because the boss in charge feels threatened by each successive comptroller's superior knowledge. But instead of admitting this weakness, he ignores it and continues his quest for a comptroller incapable of bruising his fragile ego. Most recently, Mr. Broken Collarbone fired a comptroller who, within six months of his hiring, vastly improved a problem that has caused the company to flounder for YEARS. Does this make sense to you? It shouldn't.

The real root of the revolving door of comptroller turnover (with little-to-no transition) is a technology issue forcing company employees to work around it manually. This is what happens: The new comptroller identifies the specific IT faux pas that should be rectified, but the higher-up boss dreads dealing with technical problems. The discipline and time necessary to fix the problem evokes a disruptive type of pain for Mr. Broken Collarbone, so he avoids the situation altogether by hiring and firing comptrollers. His behavior has caused the company's skeletal system not just to weaken but SHRINK. It's as if the company is a balloon he's squeezing, but because there's no opening, all the air in the balloon bulges endlessly from one end to the other. The balloon's structure can endure just so much of his squeeze-toy manipulation. When the balloon finally bursts, business bones will scatter everywhere.

And actually, there's even more trouble in my client's industrial-manufacturing paradise. The signs are everywhere: the leadership refuses to invest in their infrastructure; revenues are flat; people are fired with no regard for the transition process; the CEO focuses solely on cash flow, but doesn't care how his people make it happen. The company is about to suffer multiple broken bones and end up in a body cast. Supposedly, it's good luck to tell an actor or actress in a Broadway show to "break a leg" as a way of warding off a bad performance or the "evil eye." In the business world, falling and breaking a leg, or worse, a hip bone, isn't good luck. It indicates poor structural health. Hoping that your company's structure and infrastructure remain strong with minimal effort on your part is a bad strategy. Invest in your business bones—all 206 or so of them (350 bones if your business is a "newborn").

Chapter Ten: The Respiratory System (Endurance, Your Legs)

How many business books have you read in which one of the chapters began with a Pink Floyd song? I'll take a risk and guess the answer is "none." (Yes, I'm a huge fan of Pink Floyd's music.) Here are the perfect lyrics with which to begin our discussion of your business's respiratory fitness: "Breathe, breathe in the air. Don't be afraid to care... ("Breathe" from the 1973 album *Dark Side of the Moon*). As a business owner or CEO, you need to do a lot of deep breathing if you intend to be in business for a long time. And yes, another album and song come to mind. This time I'm relying on the wisdom of 1979's *The Long Run* by The Eagles: "You can go the distance. We'll find out in the long run." Okay, enough of DJ Brad's album collection. Let's find out if you have the aerobic capacity to ensure your company's longevity.

Surely you know that you build a sustainable business by optimizing its potential for long-term growth. The best analogy I can think of between a human body and your business's body is to ask you to visualize your company as a long-distance runner. You need stamina to be able to compete profitably in your particular industry or niche. For a long-distance runner, success in competition requires endurance training, which we'll get to momentarily. There are intangible and tangible assets that contribute to your company's respiratory fitness. The intangibles include things such as your history, reputation (dare I call it your track record?), and continuity. The tangibles include your ability to produce useful products or services upon which you can build your business's future. And the more money you make, the longer you can remain in the race. But don't be in a rush to build the staying power needed for your endless marathon. You do remember the Aesop's fable "The Tortoise and the Hare," don't you?

In the story, the Hare had so much contempt for Tortoise's lack of speed that after dashing off at the beginning of their race, Mr. Hare settled in for a nice nap. Unfortunately, he woke up just in time to see Mr. Tortoise approaching the finish line. No amount of four-pawed swiftness could help the Hare make up his lost, dawdled time, and the Tortoise won the race. While the lesson of "slow and steady wins the race" is an age-old tale, it should make sense to you regarding the best way of building business endurance. Year after year, you must develop and re-evaluate worthwhile products and services while also hiring and retaining exceptional people. You solidify the tangibles and intangibles that will keep your business moving forward during both profitable and lean times. When your business's durability is strong, clients are at their most loyal during a weak or uncertain economy. You reward that loyalty by making whatever concessions (in pricing and features) that allow you and your business to do right by these folks. Be in it for the long race, not the short race!

Part of preparing your business for long-distance running does involve your circulatory speed (as discussed in Chapter Seven). A healthy business circulation determines how quickly information and processes move through an organization. But your business won't be able to finish the race (getting a new product to market, launching an important marketing campaign or sales initiative) without a steady supply of "oxygen." Your business lungs need to be clear to inhale and exhale well. Inside your physical lungs, small tubes called bronchioles end in tiny air sacs, the alveoli. Through diffusion, oxygen moves from the alveoli and into your bloodstream by way of your capillaries. As oxygenated blood flows back to your heart, it's then pumped throughout your body. Are you maximizing your business's oxygen intake for long-term growth?

Long-distance runners get into "the zone" because they are never oxygen-depleted. They have a quick cardiovascular recovery rate and strong legs. The key to a runner's aerobic endurance is an open respiratory system. In business terms, endurance is your willingness to invest in marketing research and technology, give people the training they need to succeed, solve a customer's business problem, and stay trim by avoiding business "fat." Be sure your business avoids slipping into "sprint mode" when training for long distances.

Sprinters and long-distance runners all want to win their races, but they train for their anticipated success by following different programs. You want your business to endure unanticipated slow times while steadily building a loyal clientele. So, reduce the stress on your (business) knees, calves, and feet by avoiding the sprinter's short bursts of energy. Endurance training is all about increasing your aerobic capacity, not your muscle mass. A long-distance runner works on getting his or her heart rate elevated within a small, controlled range during trial runs and competitive races. Similarly, you must spread out exertion of energy to extend your business's longevity. Again, a healthy circulation is one of your allies against getting winded and tiring too quickly. Oxygen must be distributed properly. Always be on guard against a pulmonary embolism or other breathing ailment developing in your business lungs.

Please take a deep breath and let it out—I don't want to alarm you. A pulmonary embolism is the medical term for a sudden blockage in a lung artery. According to the National Heart, Lung and Blood Institute, "The blockage usually is caused by a blood clot that travels to the lung from a vein in the leg ... pulmonary embolism most often is a complication of a condition called deep vein thrombosis (DVT)." These blood clots develop in your body's deep veins. When the blood clot breaks loose from a vein's wall and starts to travel, your lungs are usually the final destination. It's a good idea to get up from your seat and not sit for long periods of time so a DVT blot clot doesn't develop in the first place.

Other lung conditions that can leave your business breathless include chronic obstructive pulmonary disease (also known as COPD—the two main types are chronic bronchitis and emphysema), emphysema caused by long-term cigarette smoking, and asthma. I'm not a real doctor, so if you have any concerns about any of these respiratory illnesses, please consult your physician.

Your respiratory function is a reflex that is continuous, which is why you should never hold your breath for too long. When you do this, carbon dioxide (the waste product of your exhalation) builds up inside your lungs and bloodstream with no release valve. Guess what happens next? Either you're forced to breathe, or you pass out. This is not good for your business brain—you need it to be sharp and functioning at 100%, so keep breathing. When your business body's other systems are working correctly, you create ideal conditions for maximum intake of oxygen. Businesses with longevity are proactive (e.g., product and service improvements, adjustments due to economic turndown, personnel changes, etc.) and have the energy to sustain this type of behavior.

Business endurance also ties back to your vision for the company. You don't want to be like Forrest Gump, running back and forth from one U.S. coast to the other several times (for 3 years, 2 months, 14 days, and 16 hours) just to stop running and then wonder, "What's next?" Companies with excellent business endurance foster a culture within that is always looking for the next great idea. CEOs and owners of such companies encourage their people to be innovative—they reward ingenuity and creative ideas. A company that truly demonstrates how to create and sustain business endurance is the Minnesota Mining and Manufacturing Company (3M).

In 1968, a research scientist at 3M named Dr. Spencer Silver developed an unusual adhesive. The compound had tiny spheres that didn't dissolve or melt. Each little molecule was quite sticky, yet the adhesive didn't hold strongly enough when applied to a piece of tape. No one knew what to do with this puzzling invention until 1974. This is when another 3M research scientist, Art Fay, tinkered with the adhesive and applied a strip of it to the bookmark in his church hymnbook. He wanted to see if adding the adhesive would prevent the darn thing from slipping out. Mr. Fay's "temporary permanent bookmark" evolved into the Post-it note, and the rest is endurance history.

Perhaps 3M's stock price doesn't wildly spike upward, but the company issues dividends to its stockholders year after year. Businesses like 3M are here now, and you know they will be here in the future. Companies with ample breathing capacity know when to cut bad ideas and don't have to waste time figuring out how to fix internal processes and systems. Their leaders are proactive and maintain good operational health. A healthy business prepares for its "races" just like a long-distance runner. Get your running shoes on and train with me to go the distance with your own business.

Look, the only constant you can count on is change. The changes you implement within your company should be made for the sake of improving your (People-Process-Technology) bottom line. It may not always seem necessary—change isn't easy. Running long distances can initially be painful, but then one day, it's not painful at all. This is because you've reached the crossing-over moment when your commitment to improving your personal and business health begins to stick. By surrounding yourself with employees who are "aerobically" fit and want to be members of your "running club," your business will endure. Let's take a long practice run to find out if your products or services are viable for right now and in the future.

One essential thing you must do to build strong business lungs is to ensure you have a product or service with strong demand. I know it sounds obvious, but there needs to be a need! I urge you never to fall in love so deeply with your own product or service that you become blind to its weaknesses and imperfections. Smart business owners understand their product or service must meet a need and not first be in search of consumer demand. Sadly, I know more than a few entrepreneurs who ignore this deceptively simple rule. If there is no demand for your product, you must make corrections to address the issue. When product demand is strong, it's great for your and your business, but make sure the need it satisfies is solid and sustainable. I encourage you to become familiar with the concept of "minimum viable product" and apply it to your product-development process.

According to Wikipedia, "...the minimum viable product (MVP) is a strategy used for fast and quantitative market testing of a product or product feature ... an MVP has just those features that allow the product to be deployed, and no more." Never stop making tweaks and improvements to your business offerings if doing so keeps demand going strong this year, next year, and all the years to follow. If you oversee a professional service, safeguard your company's continuance by being on time (for service calls, for client conference calls, with project deadlines) and providing great customer service so your clients will sing your praises. As long as they don't break into an "a cappella" version of the song "Long-Distance Runaround" (from the 1971 album *Fragile* by Yes), customers should be pleased with your efforts to meet and exceed their expectations. But of course, good business vision contributes to your respiratory fitness.

No, I'm not going to ask you to "breathe through your eyelids ... like the lava lizards of the Galapagos Islands" as Annie Savoy asked "Nuke" LaLoosh to do in the movie *Bull Durham*. But if you think it will help your professional vision, go right ahead. This is a gentle reminder for you to share your vision with your employees so they can see it too. You are the captain of the ship—you are responsible for charting what lies ahead for you and your employees. By not knowing the path for your business, I guarantee your people will veer off course and end up running on a rocky trail meant for mountain biking. Cultivate a healthy respiratory capacity that communicates to your fellow runners, "I know where I'm going (with our products or services)."

Also, listen to your customers. Ask them what they think of your product or service and be prepared to accept their feedback. If the people you're talking to are your best, most loyal customers, their honest feedback will probably be given with much affection. If you want the unvarnished truth, you should pay attention to all that is posted and shared about your company on social media. People really don't self-censor much on most of the online platforms—face their feedback, absorb it, and process it. One listening tool for your consideration is Klout. Your Klout score (on a scale of 1-100) represents your online influence and is calculated daily based on your activity signals coming from the various social networks: Facebook, Twitter, Google+, Foursquare, LinkedIn, etc. Because a strong social-media presence is expected nowadays, your Klout score is one way to confirm how engaging (or not) your business is online. Also hold weekly meetings to discuss what's being said about your company online and offline. Knowing the vibe your company pushes out into communities both physical and virtual helps to determine when to adjust your product offerings.

And just because your business makes good money or hits critical mass doesn't mean you stop listening to your customers. Loyalty is a two-way street. Businesses without steady respiratory fitness aren't on the receiving end of consumer affection. Companies that think their consumers are stupid are stupid companies. Perhaps you think that sounds harsh, but it's my honest opinion, and it happens to be true. Need an example from Doctor Brad's circular file? Hmm, how about the Comcast Corporation (also known as XFINITY®) of Philadelphia, Pennsylvania?

Get your fire-retardant suits on, ladies and gentlemen, because I'm about to spray Comcast's customer-service practices with an oxygen-killing flamethrower. We all know this is a mammoth-sized company. Comcast is the largest cable company and home Internet service provider in the U.S. But despite the company's longevity and growth by acquisition, Comcast's customer-service department "breathes" with the assistance of a ventilator. If you happen to be a Comcast subscriber (like me), I know you probably renegotiate your account every six months, and you get hit with new rates more often than the Philadelphia 76ers win basketball games. Wanting a strong, reliable Internet connection at home or crystal-clear cable reception shouldn't require you to play "Whack-a-Mole" every time you call Comcast.

In 2010, readers of a consumer-centric blog called The Consumerist bestowed upon Comcast the "Worst Company in America" award. There are also websites with URLs such as comcastsucks.org and comcastwatch.com. And there are even Facebook pages for you to follow called "I hate Comcast" and "Comcast Sucks!" All I'm saying is that you shouldn't have to battle with a company if you've been a loyal user of their products or services.

In a somewhat different scenario, Capital One had a reputation in the 1990s and early 2000s for marketing their credit cards to subprime customers whose credit scores were not particularly robust. There were many complaints during this time period regarding late fees and how interest was calculated for these consumers. Treating customers in a less-than-respectful manner or using slightly deceptive business practices is no way to build your company's reputation. Okay, let's get back to how you can sustain your company's products and services over time.

As I mentioned in The Circulatory System, without cash flow, endurance is impossible to sustain. A healthy circulation allows you to continually figure out how to make things better within your business. Bring in people who think strategically and aren't afraid to tell you that your bad ideas shouldn't be made. Spunky employees will steer you away from mistakes and looming disaster—they too want the company to live long (and prosper). Whatever your company is doing right, turn it into a system (i.e., some type of repetitive model). Your (tangible or intangible) strength is what differentiates and separates you from your competitors. It puts you in front, which is where you want to be for a long time. But don't get comfortable out in front. When long-distance runners become complacent with their pace or mileage, they push themselves to the next level—they make adjustments to strive for improvement. As a business "runner," you too must tinker with your product offerings to ensure customer happiness for as long as you keep breathing. And don't forget, how you market and promote your company's brand also impacts sustained endurance.

Here's where I hit you with a conflict statement regarding the best way to build an enduring brand people will remember (and perhaps even cherish). You should keep it fresh, but you should also keep it traditional. I'll explain my statement with an example. If I describe a logo that looks like a curvy, happy, yellow "M" and is referred to as the "golden arches," I know that you know the logo belongs to the McDonald's Corporation. Brothers Dick and Mac McDonald started their hamburger and barbeque business back in 1940 in San Bernardino, California. The original logo evolved from a mascot named "Speedee" to a mascot named "Archy" (and sometimes, small golden or red arches were included). But once Ray Kroc purchased exclusive rights to the McDonald's name in 1961 from Dick and Mac, the two yellow arches atop all the franchise restaurants became the dominating visual in the company's logo. Since the late 1960s, McDonald's has tinkered with the size and coloration of its "M," but the company will never abandon it. Long-term marketing of your business is like a sliding scale—you must know where you are on the scale.

When the Coca Cola Company introduced its (perceived) radical change that was New Coke in 1985 (for the detailed discussion, please revisit Chapter Four), it blew up in the leadership's faces. But when Apple transformed cell phone "button-pushers" into an army of smartphone "screen-swipers," its iPhone was considered extremely fresh. And it was easily adopted as part of the paradigm shift from desktop and laptop computers to mobile technology. You need to know your product and the

115

marketplace intimately and be tuned in to what your clients and customers want or don't want. Think of my "fresh versus tradition" paradox as your brand's sliding scale. Some consumers are eager for fresh products and marketplace change. Some of them only want basic, traditional product features. As long as you're providing consumers with consistent quality, small, non-threatening changes will eventually be accepted by even your most "old-school" customers.

Here's a great example of being nimble enough to transform a traditional product's collapse into a profitable branding redirect: the Schering-Plough Corporation's rebranding efforts for St. Joseph's Aspirin for Children back in 1993. There was a long decline in sales after pediatricians established a correlation (in the mid-1980s) between Reye's syndrome and children who were given the tiny, orange-flavored, chewable tablets to treat viral infections like chicken pox and influenza. The product was shelved in 1986. But Schering-Plough reintroduced St. Joseph's Aspirin in 1993 via samples with redeemable coupons, radio spots, and print advertising. The company rebranded it as a low-dosage, safe way for baby boomers (with childhood memories of the chewable aspirin) to reduce the risk of heart attack and stroke. When Johnson & Johnson bought the St. Joseph's brand in the early 2000s, they ratcheted up marketing of the product to adults and seniors with television commercials. The tagline for the initial commercial was "Trust it with all your heart." A very traditional product that's been around since 1887 is now a daily regimen (81 milligrams, to be exact) for adult cardiovascular care. See, change can be good for your company's respiratory fitness!

Another company that didn't abandon tradition but had enough marketing sense to assimilate technological shifts into its product line is Disc Makers (of Pennsauken, New Jersey). Disc Makers has been around since 1946. The company's website gives a hat-tip to its ability to honor tradition while staying at the front of innovation: "…From 78s to DVDs." The company came to be because of founder Ivin Ballen's love of music. Disc Makers has transitioned through a multitude of recording formats since its founding (45 vinyl singles, 33 1/3 vinyl albums, 8-track tapes and audio cassettes). When the compact-disc format was introduced in 1986, the company was there at the beginning, selling CDs in small-quantity batches by 1988. Similarly, Disc Makers adapted when the DVD format for films and DVD burners surfaced in the early 2000s. The company proclaims on its website that "Today, Disc Makers stands alone as the undisputed leader in optical disc manufacturing for independent artists, filmmakers, and businesses." Disc Makers's product-development efforts remain elastic in response to the reality of how its business niche continues to evolve.

The key take-home regarding these examples of successful endurance is that your business can't exist in a bubble from company inception onward. You must be ready to identify changes in the marketplace and adapt before your competitors. Yes, I'm nagging you again to keep your business ears open and "low to the ground." Experiment with focus groups before committing dollars to a new product or service. Go out in public and talk with consumers. Field marketing studies and track the pulse of what's going on in your market segment, using all your senses and online technology.

The different methods I'm encouraging you to use will build endurance and keep your business breathing deeply. Just make sure you're breathing from your diaphragm muscle (it's in between your ribcage and stomach), not your chest. No shallow breathing is allowed when you train with me. Abdominal breathing is the best way to slow yourself down, relieve stress, and oxygenate your body before you start you next long-distance workout. Are you ready to run this chapter's final race with me? I'm going to tell you a story about a "Big Blue" company with enough endurance to compete in consecutive Ironman (triathlon) World Championships in Kailua-Kona, Hawaii (a grueling race consisting of a 2.5 open-water swim, 112-mile bike ride, and a full 26-mile marathon run).

Chapter Ten Story:
When I graduated from college in the early 1980s, the International Business Machines Corporation (IBM) ruled the mainframe computer kingdom. And then new players, such as Microsoft and Apple, entered the personal-computer scene. IBM put together and cranked out PC "boxes" with its logo on them that contained the relatively new Microsoft's operating system, Windows, inside. Another 1980s start-up, the Dell Computer

Corporation, started manufacturing PC clones (i.e., IBM-compatible PCs). The PC market became flooded with so many choices. Tech-savvy tinkerers started building their own computers. IBM remained confident in its mainframe-systems history. But when it moved on to PCs, the company wasn't offering much that was innovative. The smaller "baby computer" companies could change and adapt to consumers' computing needs more quickly and nimbly.

IBM was moving slower than a blue-tongued skink (it's a lizard) and "turning blue in the face" by holding its breath. By 1993, the company posted a record $8 billion (annual) net loss. Everyone assumed Big Blue would vaporize into the wild blue yonder. But 1993 was also the year when Louis Gerstner, Jr., a C-level executive formerly with American Express and RJR Nabisco, joined IBM as its chairman and CEO. He was the first top leader ever brought in from outside the organization.

Mr. Gerstner had some tough decisions to face almost immediately—he knew IBM needed to "innovate or die" if it was going to stick around and endure into the 21st century. So what happened to Big Blue's sluggish mastodon of a machine? The company eliminated its hardware offerings (PCs, computer chips, etc.) and began providing its clients with knowledge and expertise rather than physical products. Instead of denying they were trapped within a saturated market, Mr. Gerstner and his executive peers made a bold change to ensure IBM's existence for a long time. And in the many years since its near-death experience, IBM continued to grow as a provider of integrated business solutions by acquiring other IT companies. By maintaining the company as a whole unit and retaining its "blue" branding, IBM managed to hold onto its traditional identity while becoming the number-one seller of IT service solutions and enterprise systems in the world. It's the new IBM, but it's still IBM.

Just about every major business school in the U.S. uses IBM as a case study and model of positive change in the corporate world. IBM is a company that understands how to expand its aerobic capacity. In the long-distance race called business competition, you train each day by tinkering, by experimenting purposefully with innovation. If a large behemoth of a company like IBM can find its way back to being a lean running machine, you and your company can do the same. That's enough reading for now. Change into your running shorts and moisture-wicking T-shirt, lace up your running shoes, and fortify your company's endurance with some leg-pumping, long-distance training. Continue to breathe in and out, deeply and continually.

Chapter Eleven: The Immune System

According to touropia.com, "Walls have been built since ancient times, to mark borders, to keep enemies out or to keep people in." The Great Wall of China, all 5,500 miles of it, took a long time to build (between the 5th century BC and the 16th century) and protected the Chinese Empire's most northern borders from aggressive nomadic tribes. Way back in AD 122, the Romans built Hadrian's Wall (this one took only 6 years to erect) across northern England (spanning 73 miles from the North Sea to the Irish Sea) to discourage the heathen clans of Scotland from invading the colony of Britannia. And then there's the Berlin Wall, constructed in 1961(and torn down in 1989) to prevent the citizens of Soviet-controlled East Berlin from escaping into West Berlin and West Germany's democratic way of life. So what the heck is the significance of all these famous walls when discussing your business's immune system? It's all about this system being your strongest line of defense against the ravages of both physical and corporate disease.

Here is a good working definition from livescience.com: "The immune system protects the body against disease or other potentially damaging foreign bodies. When functioning properly, the immune system identifies and attacks a variety of threats, including viruses, bacteria and parasites, while distinguishing them from the body's own healthy tissue." The intriguing thing about the human immune system is that it doesn't consist of one self-contained organ in the body. Also known as the lymphatic system, your immune system is a sophisticated defense mechanism consisting of bone marrow (where white blood cells are produced), the spleen, the thymus (the T-cells mature here—they assist in destroying infections and cancer cells), and lymph nodes. This is one vigilant system that never rests!

I can't proceed without mentioning an insanely favorite movie of mine, *Fantastic Voyage*. Many people mistakenly believe the 1966 film was based on a novel by Isaac Asimov, but it turns out he wrote a novelization (directly from the shooting script) that was released six months before the movie. The film's voyage is indeed fantastic, even if some of the special effects are outdated. Upon arrival in the U.S., Cold War scientist (and defector) Jan Benes suffers a stroke during a suspicious car accident and is taken by military staff to the underground headquarters of the Combined Miniature Deterrent Forces (CMDF). The CMDF commander decides to miniaturize a submarine to microscopic size so that a team of doctors can be injected into the scientist's body to remove the resulting blood clot in his brain from within.

From the IMDb website: "The problem: if they stay in longer than 60 minutes, they will grow to a size that the immune system will notice, and Benes's own defenses will mobilize to destroy them." This was heady stuff when I was a young movie-watcher! Even better, Raquel Welch is on board as a medical assistant (Cora Peterson) who's attacked by antibodies inside the patient's left ear after helping to clear the submarine of "reticular fibers." Despite any scientific inaccuracies in "Fantastic Voyage" (and there were quite a few, which Asimov amended in his novelization), you may never witness a more thrilling demonstration of the human immune system in action.

The business version of the immune system protects your company against unwanted attacks and invasions that prevent it from working properly. Are you truly aware of all the internal and external factors that can compromise your business body and cause illness (i.e., problems)? There are many germs eager to infect your company: employee theft of property, litigation, and theft (and duplication) of trade secrets or a unique business process are several likely microbes. Sometimes the most challenging illness to prevent from spreading across your company is internal strife. This disease can either build slowly or happen rapidly when one division or department literally stops your company from functioning as a whole. A variation is when two departments are locked in a power struggle that weakens your entire business. Infighting, jealousy between departments (or employees), and office politics can "kill off" the white blood cells that repel disease. The strength of your business's immune system is vital to overall health.

When a business's immune system is deficient, your company can be woefully vulnerable to attacks that sap strength and weaken performance. These attacks can do just as much damage when inflicted by either an individual or a staff of people. Let's say you have a great employee who feels he or she is never heard and whose advice or suggestions are never acted upon. Don't be surprised when that employee leaves to work elsewhere. And don't be shocked when other talented people also start submitting their two-week notices. Your immune system weakens with each departing employee. If your business's bone marrow starts producing too many abnormal white blood cells and leukemia (cancer of the blood) develops, no matter how strong your business muscles are, you won't be able to fight off the impact on the other systems in your business body.

When your immune system is compromised, the overall burden on your other business systems becomes painfully noticeable. Your circulatory system will probably take a hit as cash flow begins to dry up. And without the strength to fight off illness, your respiratory system will have a hard time providing the business oxygen needed to ensure your company's endurance and longevity. Please don't force me to tell you what happens to your digestive system when your business defenses are depleted. One key factor that provokes the immune system is stress. Similar to the way stress can hammer away at your physical body, a high-stress work environment isn't good for your business processes or your people. Business owners who psychologically pressure their employees may elicit good or even great results, but it's an exhausting way to work. There's a difference between slaving away in a high-pressure zone versus working in a zone of brilliance.

I can't take credit for the concept I'm about to share with you—I'm referencing an interesting book by psychologist Gay Hendricks called *The Big Leap*. In his book, the author identifies four primary zones in which we all function: the Zones of

Incompetence, Competence, Excellence, and Genius. Once in the Zone of Excellence, you do what you do extremely well, but you're capable of doing more. My opinion is that if you're not thriving, you're settling for the status quo. You get tired, which leads to stress and a possibly compromised immune system. You want your company functioning in the Zone of Genius, where all barriers and fears are removed. Tapping into your strongest, most innate talent is liberating because it leaves you exhilarated, not tired. If you're not ready to lead your people into the Zone of Genius, you haven't yet reinforced all the weak spots in your business's immune system.

That old cliché "a chain is only as strong as its weakest link" is a great analogy when evaluating your business immune system. These are just a few of the weak links that can allow business germs to infiltrate your body: lack of investment in your people, not taking care of contracts, not keeping accurate, up-to-date accounting books and other corporate records, and no protection of intellectual property. The list is endless. When your attention is distracted from the legal and financial duties of running a business, you literally pay for it when faced with penalties and fines on the back end. These details should be locked up and heavily protected by corporate white blood cells. One of the most unnerving threats your business's immune system can face is when your IT system and data are violated. On December 18, 2013, security expert Brian Krebs (krebsonsecurity.com) revealed one of the worst attacks on a company's immune system in history: the Target holiday-shopping credit card and debit card breach.

According to many print and online sources, the actual hacking into Target's customer database happened between November 27 and December 15 of that year. Initially, Target stated that upward of 40 million customer credit and debit cards were possibly compromised. Then in January 2014, the company admitted the number of people affected by this security disaster was closer to 110 million. And get this—the suspected programmer was a Russian teenager! This clever boy developed and sold a point-of-sale malware program that hackers used to creep into Target's customer database the way a (rare) brain-eating amoeba can enter the human body (via the nose, mouth, or ears) and destroy brain tissue. Is that vivid enough for you? Target's IT system may be patched, but it's going to take a long time for the company's reputation to heal as far as customers are concerned. When your IT security is fragile and exposed to unknown viruses, it may pick up a nasty MRSA infection. This is not a good thing.

For those of you who are unaware, Methicillin-resistant Staphylococcus aureus (MRSA) infections occur most frequently in hospitals or other health care facilities. But germs reside everywhere in the environment. You could become the host site for a viral or bacterial infection while riding a plane, train, bus, or enormous cruise ship. The problem with catching a MRSA infection is that this particular strain of staph bacteria is incredibly resistant to many of the antibiotics used to treat it. And the people most likely to encounter MRSA are hospital patients recovering from surgery as well as those with a weakened immune system. Most staph infections start as skin infections that find an opening (literally) and work their way into the human body before the real damage occurs.

With a deficient business immune system, all it takes is one little scratch (like lack of communication) or a surgical wound (like employee apathy) to let the bad germs in. When businesses get sick, people start looking for a healthier work environment, and companies become vulnerable merger or acquisition candidates. Once a "superbug" enters your business body, the company may not be strong enough to fight it off. You may not even realize what's happening. There are so many environmental variables that create the viruses and bacteria in search of a warm place to breed and take over. Perhaps it's time for your company to "innovate or die."

Relax—I'm not suggesting you allow your business to be invaded by a superbug. I'm merely referencing a 1996 book by Jack V. Matson, a professor at Penn State University. The book's full title is *Innovate or Die! A Personal Perspective on the Art of Innovation.* Per innovateordieonline.com, Professor Matson "...centers his techniques on teaching people to unlearn years of practicing risk aversion by stressing the connection between creativity, innovation, and risk." Innovation doesn't necessarily mean a product or service—changing the way you run your business and interact with your employees may be all the innovation you need to build up your business's immune system. Let's revisit your white blood cells and discuss strategies for keeping your immune system strong.

Although white blood cells account for only 1% of your human blood (the other elements being red blood cells, platelets, and plasma), they are your strongest allies against disease and infection. In the business world, I consider you, the owner or CEO of a company, to be the white blood cells. You ward off illness with your effective leadership and management skills. But are you producing enough healthy cells? The only way to be sure is by testing your white blood cell count regularly to check for warning signs of infection.

In the medical world, the test to monitor your white blood cells is called a complete blood count. If the count is too high or too low, this might be an indication of disease or illness. According to the University of Rochester Medical Center website, "Your white blood cell count can be low for a number of reasons—when something is destroying the cells more quickly than the body can replenish them or when the bone marrow stops making enough white blood cells to keep you healthy. When your white blood cell count is low, you are extremely susceptible to any illness or infection, which can spiral into a serious health threat." Part of your job is to monitor your company's internal defenses.

By checking your white blood cell levels regularly and keeping track of whether your count is good or dropping, you'll know when something is wrong with your business body. If you're fighting off an attack, activate the protective systems you have in place—your lawyer, your accountant, drug-testing of employees, product quality-control processes—to safeguard your immune system. But you don't always have to be on the defense. Remember, a strong immune system never sleeps. As the main "producer" of white blood cells in your business body, you must enforce procedures that encourage positive growth and change.

Providing open forms of communication (such as town-hall meetings and creativity workshops) as well as decent employment benefits are good ways of warding off personnel epidemics. Monitoring the health of your internal processes by conducting financial audits and legal compliance reviews is vital. Product or service reviews and creation of improvement schedules with clear milestones generate the kind of blood cells your company needs to thrive in your industry. And that old saying about feeding a cold and starving a fever? Never starve your business systems or people—feed them!

I'll address the fever thing first. These songs are bound to raise your temperature a bit: "Fever" (original version by Little Willie John, iconic version covered by Peggy Lee), "Jungle Fever" (by the universally respected Stevie Wonder), "Cat Scratch Fever" (a blatantly sexual ditty by Ted Nugent—meow!), and "Night Fever" (by The Bee Gees, during the 1970s' disco days). But the song I'm saving for last is Bruce Springsteen's "The Fever." If you don't heed a business infection and treat it properly, you'll have to accept this warning (from one "Boss" to another): "…The fever gets worse every day." What are you going to do about the fever spreading throughout your business? If I were you, I'd take the advice of a certain lawn-obsessed Scotsman…

Yes, I'm about to dispense sound business advice using the spokesman for Scotts Turf Builder® lawn products as my inspiration. In case you didn't know, a burly-yet-friendly Scotsman named Scott (also known as Phil McKee, an Edinburgh-based character actor) became the public face of Scotts, the lawn-care company, in 2012. Since then, his primary goal has been to encourage homeowners to maintain their lawns by using the company's products. When Scott from Scotts isn't busy training his wee Scottie of a dog, Haggis, he proclaims advice I suggest you apply to your business body: "Your grass, man, it's a living, breathing thing … It's hungry, and you've got to feed it." Feed your company's immune system to keep it healthy.

Good business nutrition means you invest (yes, you do have to pay for it) in actionable training and education as well as off-site retreats and events to which your employees can invite their family members. If you like and respect people enough to work with them, you should be willing to play and also do volunteer work with them. In humans, protein consumed from both animal and vegetable sources creates muscle. In businesses, the protein you should be feeding your people is accurate, aggregated, measurable data. Business intelligence becomes a form of biofeedback your employees can use to regulate their particular responsibilities and make good decisions. You've got to feed your business in real time when the information is needed most or its blood sugar will drop. Before you know it, your company is hypoglycemic and doesn't have enough energy to function properly. Starving your business is a very bad idea.

Without proper nutrition, your business's cash flow will dry up. The company will become emaciated and weak. On the other end of the feeding spectrum, if your business stops exercising and becomes lazy, innovation stops, and the organization gets bloated. Once a business is overweight and out of shape, too much fat enters the blood stream, which compromises the immune system. One way to enhance your company's nutritional intake and boost the immune system's defenses is by supplementing with the business equivalent of a probiotic.

Unless you never watch television, you know by now that probiotics are live microorganisms (referred to as "good bacteria" or yeast) consumed to aid digestive and intestinal health. And Dr. Mehmet Oz says that "Furthermore, probiotics can provide multiple benefits for your immune system. When probiotics are abundant in your body, it's harder for bacteria that cause illness to get a foothold." You could add more yogurt to your diet or a take a probiotic supplement (like Align® or Florastor®) to help strengthen your physical immune system. I suggest you also "consume" business probiotics to target those areas of weakness within your company in need of better protection.

If you've skated by without an employee handbook for years because you never had a dedicated HR staff member, outsource the task to an HR consultant. Your business is booming but corporate clients are hurting your cash flow? Then apply for a line of credit. Are you panicked by the news you read about hackers unleashing yet another computer bug or virus into the public domain that might infiltrate your computer technology? Then hire an IT specialist to add more security to your servers and systems. By surrounding a deficiency with extra resources, you safeguard your entire immune system.

Is your company weak with fever from a recurring infection? You might need the ultimate business probiotic: a turnaround specialist. This is a highly specialized consultant who "nurses" struggling or failing businesses back to health. A turnaround specialist will "eat" the bad bacteria in your business body (firing infectious employees, cutting projects that do nothing but suck up money) while introducing the necessary good bacteria (replacing a bad product-development process with a more efficient, less costly one). But your best efforts to supplement good business nutrition are sometimes no match for more serious health issues like a business organ transplant or an autoimmune disease.

When a company contemplates merging with a competitor or acquiring another company, the biggest fear is that things won't come together. Just like a kidney or liver transplant in a human can be rejected by the recipient's body, you face the possibility of a failed merger if the two different business cultures reject each other instead of reaching acceptance. Some of the most epic, spectacularly bad business mergers to result in complete organ rejection include: The Quaker Oats Company and Snapple (in 1994), AOL and Time Warner (in 2000), and Kmart and Sears (in 2005). A business transplant can be a painful (and doomed) operation, but I think even worse than a failed merger is a company living with an autoimmune disease.

I hope an autoimmune disorder never develops within your company. The reason a healthy immune system works so well is that it can distinguish between its host body and foreign invaders. But when there's a flaw and your body can't discern between "self and non-self," autoantibodies called antigens are produced that mistakenly attack normal, healthy cells. Per the womenshealth.gov website: "This causes the damage we know as autoimmune disease. The body parts that are affected depend on the type of autoimmune disease. There are more than 80 known types."

Several autoimmune diseases you may be familiar with are celiac disease (gluten intolerance), Hashimoto's disease (underactive thyroid), multiple sclerosis (attacks the myelin sheath surrounding the nervous system), and lupus (can damage your joints, skin, kidneys, heart, lungs, and other body parts). When specific employees or departments within your business are sabotaging or attacking each other, your company is already suffering from an autoimmune disease. Without proper intervention, the disease will cascade and cause harm. It will become harder and harder for your company to recover and return to good health. I just so happen to have an out-of-state client with multiple immune-system disorders…

Chapter Eleven Story:

This particular client is flipped for purchase almost every five years because the "new rules" for doing business get rejected, and the top talent leaves. The company has weakened its immune system so badly that I doubt my usual remedies will lead this client back to full health. The recurring turnover stunts the company's growth. The leaders can't seem to focus on their competition. And of course, with a not-so-reliable reputation, my client has lost more than a few sales opportunities. Throughout this company, divisions and departments are not listening to each other. More specifically, the engineering department is understaffed and has marginal resources. The people in this department have no respect for other departments they should be working with closely. And it all stems from another department's deliberate action, which in turn triggered an expensive recall.

When yet another management team cycled into the company, the engineering department was deemed inferior by the new leaders. They decided to plug in their own people and exclude the veteran engineers from an important production decision. The company, as represented by a group of engineers now viewed collectively as insignificant white blood cells, rejected the new management's plan. I suppose the transfusion of "new blood" caused these executives to assume the company's immune system was fine. But actually, production of white blood cells was building up before an internal attack. Engineering was overruled by the production department. It was only a matter of time before the company's immune system was completely compromised.

The resulting product recall was a full-blown autoimmune disorder (I'll call it Tornberg's disease) for which I couldn't prescribe any medication. Senior management had to traipse all over the U.S. to client sites and calm down the spreading fear. The product failed because management and the production staff stood by a marketing decision to substitute a more expensive part with cheaper, seven-dollar part. My client was lured into attacking what was actually a healthy organ (i.e., the engineering department) and ended up destroying too many normal cells. The company still hasn't recovered from this product recall—I honestly believe it will be gone in a few more years. Current management cleaned house (and destroyed the good bacteria in its business body) too well.

While this client's president keeps looking at the financials, he can't see the real problem: a disease (of the product-development process) that is destroying the company's defenses from within. He doesn't recognize just how all-encompassing the company's immune system is and how it impacts all the other systems in the business. Attacking your own people and leaving them as collateral damage is a bad way to run a company. Beware such self-destructive behavior. Safeguard your business immune system for optimal protection against internal and external invasions.

Chapter Twelve: The Total Business Body

Now that we've come to the final "business body" chapter, I can't help but think about a board game that's been in production since 1965: Operation. The game's official description on boardgamegeek.com says it "is a dexterity game in which you must extract silly body parts from a hapless patient." If you touch the metal sides of any body cavity when trying to remove a silly body part, the patient, Cavity Sam, cries out in pain. His nose lights up, and a silly sound flees his tortured body. The Operation dude's incredibly unhealthy body still includes wacky body parts like a wrenched ankle, a breadbasket (the stomach), and a broken heart. But if you don't have the proper dexterity to play well, you could "kill" the patient on the operating table. Thank goodness it's only a game.

Your physical body will give you much better warning signals than a red nose and burping sound when it's not doing so well. The business body also presents symptoms to let you know that its health is in decline. Ignoring indicators of an unhealthy business body is the worst possible decision you can make as a business owner or CEO. You must care for your business's health the same way you should be taking care of your physical well-being.

For example, a poor circulatory system (cash flow and the transactional processes discussed in Chapter Seven) will choke off your business endurance and ability to be agile. Business-system neglect leads to deterioration, which will definitely force you to seek "medical" attention from someone like me before the healing can begin. And if you stop communicating with your people, it's like having a pinched nerve.

Think I don't know what I'm talking about? A few years ago, I suffered a C6-C7 spinal-disc injury, also known as radiculopathy. According to spinehealth.com, this is "nerve root irritation and/or damage related to a herniated disc in your vertebrae/spinal column." I now know the pain I felt was the result of my herniated discs pressing on a cervical nerve (hence, the pinching aspect). First my wrist hurt, and then my elbow hurt, but I ignored these symptoms. I made a bad decision—and my arm strength dwindled down to 10% of its usual capacity. I ended up having a laminectomy. This is a surgical procedure to remove a ruptured or herniated disc from the back of your neck. It relieves the pressure on your cervical nerve.

When a pinched nerve is translated into business terms, degenerative communication leads to permanent harm. The loss of information literally cuts off your company's central nervous system and its ability to talk to the other organs and systems within your business body. If your cash flow is bad, pretending it's not a problem isn't the answer. You're either not billing often enough or not selling enough inventory or services. If you're limping, what's wrong? Is it your knee, your leg, or something else you're unable to diagnose on your own? It's crucial to uncover the root cause of any business-body illness or injury. Your symptoms may not indicate the actual problem. Insufficient cash flow can be a sign of poor decision-making that goes deeper than billing or inventory issues. I urge you to recognize that optimal health is the most important aspect of the business body. Only when your company is functioning at 100% can it be profitable. And a fit business (as well as business owner) attracts the right type of relationships in the business dating pool.

Ladies, this one is for you. Let's say you and some good friends walk into a popular bar that serves the latest mojito, martini, and daiquiri cocktails. As you approach the bartender to order your libation, you notice two men already enjoying their Friday night. One of them is dressed in a sharp, well-fitting suit that is possibly custom-made. He's also wearing what could be Italian loafers. The other prospect (regardless of the cash and credit cards in his wallet) is wearing frayed, ratty cargo pants, an unbuttoned flannel shirt, a Grateful Dead T-shirt underneath, and flip-flops. Be honest: which one instinctively attracts your attention? If it's bachelor number two, you definitely need Brad the Dating Doctor's help, stat. Prospective clients and customers want to "hook up" and get serious with fit, attractive companies and their owners. One of the best ways to make your business more appealing to others is by being responsive.

This leadership trait is at the top of my list. It indicates you're a good business owner or CEO. Responsiveness tells me you care about your business. Clients and customers notice when you get back to them quickly and make it easy for them to do business with you. Please don't wince as I trot out Amazon.com again as an example of a company that responds quickly and makes ordering anything online so simple. Since its early days as an online bookseller, Amazon has grown year after year. A little digging on the Business Insider website reveals that the company now sells over 100 million items in more than 30 product categories.

Amazon is a streamlined company doing everything it can to make your online shopping experience a seamless one. Customers appreciate technological innovations like Amazon's 1-Click option. Think about it: Would you rather walk into a sleepy bookstore where you can't find anyone to help you or order hard-to-locate books online in a few minutes? Amazon operates at 100% optimal health, with no real problems. Being responsive to others and fostering that type of mentality throughout your company are admirable leadership traits. And responsiveness creates a strong sense of confidence in the way you run your business.

You as an owner or CEO should care and listen. When you do, the resulting company culture demonstrates you value your clients and realize they are intrinsic to your success. It's very similar to the dating process. There are online dating services for different demographics: eHarmony, Match.com, OKCupid, Plenty of Fish, Christian Mingle, JDate (if you can't figure this one out, call or e-mail me), Zoosk, Date Hookup, and now Our Time (you have to be over 50 to play here). Business dating takes place both online (LinkedIn, Facebook, Twitter, etc.) and in the physical world. Good business relationships are all about communication and responsiveness.

Your behavior online and at meetings and business-networking events impacts a prospective customer's opinion of you and your company. But let's be real for a moment—people also like doing business with attractive candidates. When you meet another business owner or CEO who is physically fit and exudes energy, your respect for that person increases. Leaders who are rude, loud, and out of shape probably have an overabundance of employees just like them back at the office. This is no way to attract new clients and retain current clients. And be respectful of others by minding your manners. Whether you're meeting with a prospective client or longtime customer, be polite—hold your calls and silence your mobile device. Your physical actions speak volumes regarding how you manage your people and lead your company. Be an accurate reflection of your business operations. But this isn't always the case, especially in family-owned businesses.

A critical mistake these owners make all too often is not running the business as professionally as they should. And sometimes, entrepreneurship skips a generation in a family business. Not every son or daughter is destined to follow in the footsteps of his or her charismatic parent. As a disciple of all things related to *The Godfather* book and movies, I refer to this phenomenon as "The Fredo Corleone Principle." Don Vito Corleone had three sons: Santino (Sonny), Frederico (Fredo), and Michael. The adult Fredo was perceived as the weakest Corleone in his family's second generation. He usually handled relatively minor or unimportant tasks regarding the family business.

This heartbreaking quote from *The Godfather, Part II* (via imdb.com) is the reality in many a family-owned business: "I'm your older brother, Mike, and I was stepped over! ... It ain't the way I wanted it! I can handle things! I'm smart! Not like everybody says ... like dumb ... I'm smart and I want respect!" I don't have to tell you what happened to Fredo at the end of the movie, do I? The weak offspring of a strong leader is something to be monitored in a family business. Let's move on to the social aspects of getting to know your customers.

Customer Relationship Management (CRM) is a very mainstream concept these days. You cultivate your clients and customers "from cradle to grave" by monitoring information and notes stored in a database. When nurturing a prospect to your end goal of closing a deal, you work through a series of deliberate processes and actions. But these days, CRM is much more than a database filled with static customer profiles. The social aspect of customer relationships now extends beyond documenting notes in your CRM software every time you speak with customers. In today's world of mobile portability and digital content, a lot of valuable business insight is available to you through social media. If you haven't done so yet, add an "S" (for "Social") in front of "CRM." Social listening is a habit that's good for your business body.

To your face, clients and customers might offer nothing but positive feedback regarding their experiences working with you. But on a platform like LinkedIn (and more likely, Facebook or Twitter), they will reveal other facts that, while not disastrous, may be the exact feedback you need to improve a process or product. Paying attention to the information your clients post to their social-media accounts (and pulling it into your existing CRM database) provides a better picture of what motivates and repels them.

Listening via social media offers insight into the business deals your customers make, the hobbies they enjoy, and the charitable causes they champion. If you're not listening to what your customers are saying online, I guarantee your competitors are. By the time you decide to (begrudgingly) invest your time in social listening, your clients already know the benefits of working with you and what is good (or not good) about your company. If you choose not to participate in the online conversation, you'll be late to the prospecting process when it comes to new business opportunities.

Forget the "old-school" pipeline of cold-calling and walking around neighborhoods to distribute promotional flyers or brochures. Social listening is an innovative tool that can help you "get in" early before your prospective customer makes the final decision. Don't be a commodity or benchmark bid when differentiating your products or services from your competitors' offerings. You want to be the trusted advisor and authority within your niche or industry. Participating online creates strategic advantages, but you have to earn your "backstage pass" to the show.

Consider maintaining a Google account so you can be active on Google+. Google's most current attempt at social networking rewards people who engage online. Participation is good for your social reach. Google+ also helps your website's ranking on Search Engine Results Pages (SERPs) when prospects search for your business (by using Google, naturally). Curating (i.e., sharing) interesting and relevant content from other sources is good for your social-media footprint. Original content written in-house (a company blog, white papers, e-books, etc.) that educates or inspires without a "hard sell" is a great way of establishing yourself as an industry expert. The opportunity to attract eyeballs and encourage interaction is a real-time, moving target.

There are many resources available online for gathering intelligence on either customers or competitors. Test out the Technorati search engine to find blogs that might be useful in your information-collecting efforts. For those of you becoming more active on Twitter, Google+ or Instagram, experiment with sites like hashtags.org, hashtagify.me, or hashtracking.com to identify trending and useful hashtags. It's relatively easy to determine the places online where social relationships with your customers should start.

Whether your business sells merchandise, provides professional services or manufactures something, the LinkedIn platform is a great starting point for true business-related engagement. In particular, LinkedIn provides access to industry peers and potential customers through its Groups feature. All you need do is search LinkedIn for the groups that best target your social-networking goals and request to join. Then flex your knowledge of trends within your industry by contributing to LinkedIn discussions. You can participate similarly on many of the other social-media platforms where your customers and prospects dwell online. Now that I've got you interested in using social media to bolster your CRM database, you're wondering how much time all this activity requires. Let's face the issue, squarely and directly.

No matter the size of your company, feeding the social-media beast as part of your business body's daily requirements is a time investment. You can create a free account on most of the usual suspects. But time spent posting and tweeting and sharing and engaging online is time taken away from other responsibilities. Those of you who are solo entrepreneurs perhaps struggle with a dual challenge: pushing out content as well as having conversations on social media daily (as a way to "soft sell" your business). There are options available for minimizing the time suck of social media, depending on your budget.

For some of you it might make sense to outsource your social-media efforts to a local (or even remote) professional. Does your company have an internal marketing or communications department? If so, consider deeming that staff's most online-savvy individual the king or queen of your social-media activity. Another approach is to bring in an intern to handle your social-media accounts. To pursue this option, start your search with internships.com. Employers can post internship openings for free on the website. Concerns you may have regarding time needed to create original content (blog posts, articles for e-mail or newsletter blasts, white papers, etc.) are real. My philosophy is to write something once and then repurpose the content many times on social media. This eases the burden of having to crank out fresh content every day. When it comes to integrating social media into your marketing strategy, use your time wisely.

Another facet of participating online is that it's not just you looking in the digital mirror anymore. What I mean is this: With the advent of social media on the Internet, nothing (and I mean literally NOTHING) is a secret anymore. The speed of informational transactions online is a (virtual) double-edged sword. Your online footprint is readily available for the world to see: your company website, your blog(s), your Facebook page, your LinkedIn company page, and more. And it's not just your online locations that people notice. They also form early impressions of your company based on your online behavior, your followers and connections, and what you're sending out into the digital world. In other words, I'm talking about your online voice and reputation. You can never again rely only on the "good old days" of manual, analog communication.

Years ago when you lost a client or customer account, you probably just went out there and "found" another one. But in the current digital world, communication is a constantly running dialogue. Your online reputation follows you everywhere and is how others construct a full picture of your business. Companies that share meaningful posts about charitable events they host or sponsor (such as a Habitat for Humanity construction project) are viewed as being part of a credible online community. People want to connect with and admire businesses that make them feel good. Think about how you (and your employees) can represent your company to the public in a way that provides a compelling reason to revisit your online "homes." As the founder of a training organization for business owners, I intend to build its reputation in a giving way.

Established in 2013, Small Business University (SBU) offers southern New Jersey and metro Philadelphia business owners both in-person training seminars and networking opportunities on a bimonthly-to-quarterly basis. When formulating SBU, I felt strongly about establishing a relationship with a charity. I wanted SBU attendees to understand the giving element embedded in the organization's structure. And so, SBU raises money for The Sunshine Foundation, which "answers the dreams of chronically ill, seriously ill, physically challenged and abused children, ages 3-18, whose families cannot fulfill their requests, due to the financial strain that child's illness may cause." Two of my daughters spent quite a bit of time at the Children's Hospital of Philadelphia fighting their own childhood illnesses. Now you know why The Sunshine Foundation means so much to me.

My SBU team members and I are longtime professionals who are firmly established in our respective businesses. We take care to ensure our actions are aligned with SBU's overall philosophy (of giving and receiving). We would never want to inadvertently send out any mixed messages regarding our organization's goals. Too much work goes into SBU to risk losing the online community's trust and letting our reputation flounder. Looking good to outside admirers and feeling good within your company are worthy ambitions. Just be sure you make time for regular business physicals.

I've made many recommendations to you throughout our journey together (thanks for accompanying me). Here are a few final tips for optimizing your business's health. No matter how experienced your CIO, COO or other top technical leader, find an outside advisor you can trust to conduct intermittent IT reviews and internal-systems audits. Create open peer groups so employees from different departments and levels can discuss how they feel about their work, what's going well, and what isn't going too well. Basically, ask the "cooks" in your kitchen how the food tastes before serving it to your business body. Nothing stimulates your business senses more than looking within and admitting to your own blemishes. I probably said this once or twice already, but don't be afraid to hire people who understand certain processes within your company better than you do. It is a selfless, confident leader who can do this without hesitation.

On a regular basis, look at your People-Process-Technology triangle to assess how well you are fulfilling each segment's training and educational needs. Rather than hiring full-time employees and "hurling" them at your operational processes, consider bringing in business-operations consultants as needed. One tool I haven't yet mentioned regarding improvement of your company's operational health is the Six Sigma concept. If you're not familiar with Six Sigma, it's a "disciplined, data-driven approach and methodology for eliminating defects (driving toward six standard deviations between the mean and the nearest specification limit) in ANY process—from manufacturing to transactional and from product to service." There's a lot more to it than this definition from isixsigma.com, and formal Six Sigma training doesn't creep into your company's budget cheaply. You can self-educate by reading books or using Six Sigma software before applying the principles to your business. Once you educate yourself about the Six Sigma process (define, measure, analyze, design, verify), you can then introduce the concept of continuous improvement to your people.

I'm a true believer in process remediation: it can streamline systems, reduce task and transition time, and improve work habits. In my not-so-humble opinion, continuous improvement needs to be the mantra of both large and small businesses. If you sell merchandise, you should be counting your inventory every six months. For those of you handicapped by weak technical processes or staff, banish your 800-pound gorilla back to the closest zoo. Hire an IT consultant to put the correct systems in place and strengthen the "T" in your PPT triangle. But be careful—you want to improve the ideas and practices that are your company's core competencies.

Spend your money knowingly on an important process requiring significant help. For example: Perhaps your IT infrastructure hasn't been upgraded in years but, at this very moment, you have no lead-nurturing process or system in place. Rather than overspending on both headaches at the same time, prioritize and fix the problem that will boost your bottom line better. Your ability to focus effectively on your business's core competencies will increase if you follow the Pareto principle. I mentioned this earlier as the 80/20 rule (source: whatis.techtarget.com): "…a theory maintaining that 80 percent of the output from a given situation or system is determined by 20 percent of the input." Don't throw money at processes or technology that won't noticeably improve your profits—assess and prioritize first. Your yearly (or biyearly, or quarterly) business physical is critical to your company's health.

And speaking of physicals: Even if your own employees tell you that nothing is wrong, don't wait until your business is terminally ill to get the proper help. Your one clearly known problem may turn out to be multiple problems impacting other areas in your company. Don't be the last one to find out your business is on the brink of Multiple System Organ Failure (MSOF—yes, it's as bad as it sounds). This is when more than one organ in your human body no longer functions normally. According to the American Thoracic Society, "Organs can stop working, or 'fail,' for a number of different reasons. Some common reasons that cause more than one organ at a time to fail are serious infections [usually the result of sepsis], low blood pressure (called 'shock') and serious injuries (called 'trauma'). In general, the chance of a patient dying in the hospital increases each day that organs don't improve functioning." Are you aware that MSOF is the leading cause of death in a hospital's ICU?

And mull over this startling tidbit from the Centers for Disease Control and Prevention: Colonoscopy screenings for colorectal cancer (recommended starting at age 50) save lives, but one in three adults skips undergoing this life-saving diagnostic procedure. This statistic astonishes me. Some people don't understand the purpose of a colonoscopy. Some people worriedly assume the procedure is too expensive. And many people are fearful of something being found. I'd rather be proactive about my business's health (and overcome my obsessive fears) than wait too long to discover half my client base is unhappy with me. Wouldn't you? Be as proactive about your business body's health and well-being as humanly possible.

I hope you'll keep this book in your office and refer back to it intermittently. But if not, remind yourself daily that both your human and business bodies must have all systems functioning at 100% to be healthy and competitive. All the business-body systems we discussed are interdependent on one another, just as all the organs and systems in your human body interconnect and work together to keep you "alive and kicking." Neglecting your business's health by ignoring symptoms and warning signs of something gone astray is bad. Your negligence is more likely to cascade into multiple problems or weaknesses. When there's pain, you need to acknowledge it.

I'm no medical doctor, but I believe any pain your company experiences is actually good. Pain helps you diagnose the specific problems you as the top leader must face and solve before they segue into utter catastrophe. Pay attention to your People-Process-Technology triangle. Maintain it with good business nutrition and exercise. Sustain your company for as long as you'd like it to exist, thrive, and succeed. But be capable of identifying and rooting out your own flaws as a leader.

One of my favorite books is *The Art of War*, attributed to Sun Tzu, who was a high-ranking general and strategist in the Chinese army during that country's Spring and Autumn Period (approximately 722 – 481 BC). This ancient military text is divided into chapters; I constantly revisit Chapter Eight, "Variation in Tactics." I tend to share this particular principle with my clients: "There are five dangerous faults which may affect a general: (1) Recklessness, which leads to destruction; (2) cowardice, which leads to capture; (3) a hasty temper, which can be provoked by insults; (4) a delicacy of honor which is sensitive to shame; (5) over-solicitude for his men, which exposes him to worry and trouble." By minimizing the weaknesses in your leadership style, you will optimize your company's health. A fit business, a fit body, a fit mind—these are the elements that make you successful and competitive, both as a business owner and human being. So get in shape!

About the Author, Brad Tornberg:

When Brad Tornberg, Owner and Principal of E3 Consulting, preaches the gospel of business fitness, his eyes widen and his pulse quickens. He's ready to educate, enable, and empower your company to the next level. Brad knows that your business body, just like your human body, must be functioning at 100% for optimal health.

Brad possesses over 30 years of IT systems, business operations, and Customer Relationship Management (CRM) software experience. His technological expertise and command of marketing strategies are now merged into one powerful business toolbox. His unique consulting method is professional yet nurturing. Highly approachable, Brad will point out your actual problem and guide you toward a healthier, more robust way of running your organization. In other words, Brad will lead you to superior business fitness!

Because he's worked with countless CEOs, CFOs, CIOs, business owners and principals, Brad speaks your language. But he won't bewilder you with complicated techno-speak or consulting jargon. As a business owner who comes from a family of entrepreneurs, Brad understands your company's precarious balance between people, processes, and technology. His empathy for your business dilemma is surpassed only by his passion for solving it, explaining things to you simply and clearly.

Are you ready to partner with an enthusiastic troubleshooter? Brad will resolve both your infrastructure and operational issues using the skill set your business's overburdened body cries out for. If you still haven't found the shortest path to fixing your predicament (while minimizing the cost), you need a reliable, loyal business confidant. You need Brad Tornberg of E3 Consulting. Once you believe in Brad and his multi-angled approach to mending frayed companies, you will never want to let him go. Your business will be healthier, and there's a good chance you and your people will also become healthier. A fit business STAYS in business!

Brad Tornberg, Chief Business Fitness Officer (CBFO), E3 Consulting

How You Can Connect with Brad Tornberg:

Phone: 1-732-735-6429
E-mail: brad@e3help.com
Website: www.e3help.com

LinkedIn Company Page:
www.linkedin.com/company/e3-consulting-partners-llp

Google+ Company Page:
plus.google.com/105022657631185191158/posts

Twitter Business Account:
twitter.com/E3ConsultingInc

Facebook Company Page:
www.facebook.com/e3consultingpartners

LinkedIn:
www.linkedin.com/pub/brad-tornberg/5/651/b41

Google+:
plus.google.com/111090899477788446123/posts

Facebook:
www.facebook.com/brad.tornberg.3

www.ingramcontent.com/pod-product-compliance
Lightning Source LLC
Chambersburg PA
CBHW051535170526
45165CB00002B/742